Name ______________________________ Da

MW01630530

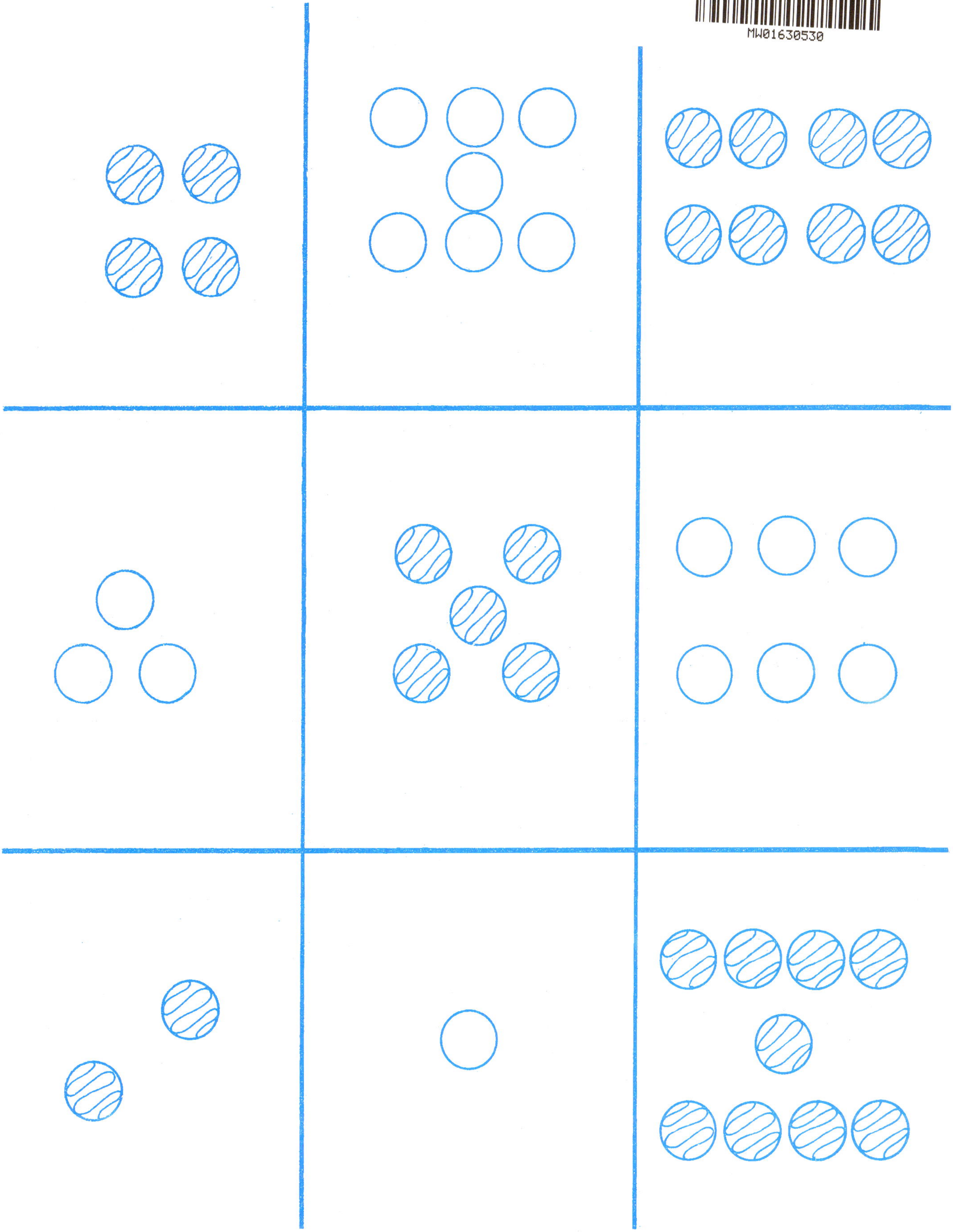

Ref: *Lab Sheet Annotations,* page 14.

Name ______________________ Date ______________

Ref: *Lab Sheet Annotations,* page 14.

Name ______________________ Date ______________

Ref: *Lab Sheet Annotations*, page 14.

Name ______________________ Date ______________

A a A	B b B b b B b B	F f
D d D d d D d	M	r R R r r
E e e e E e	G g G G	N N N n n n N N N

Ref: *Lab Sheet Annotations,* page 14.

Name ____________________ Date ____________

0	1	2	3	4	5	6	7	8	9	10

How Many?

2

6

0

7

1

5

Ref: *Lab Sheet Annotations*, page 16.

How Many?

Name ______________________

Date __________________

9	
1	
7	
4	
2	

Ref: *Lab Sheet Annotations*, page 16.

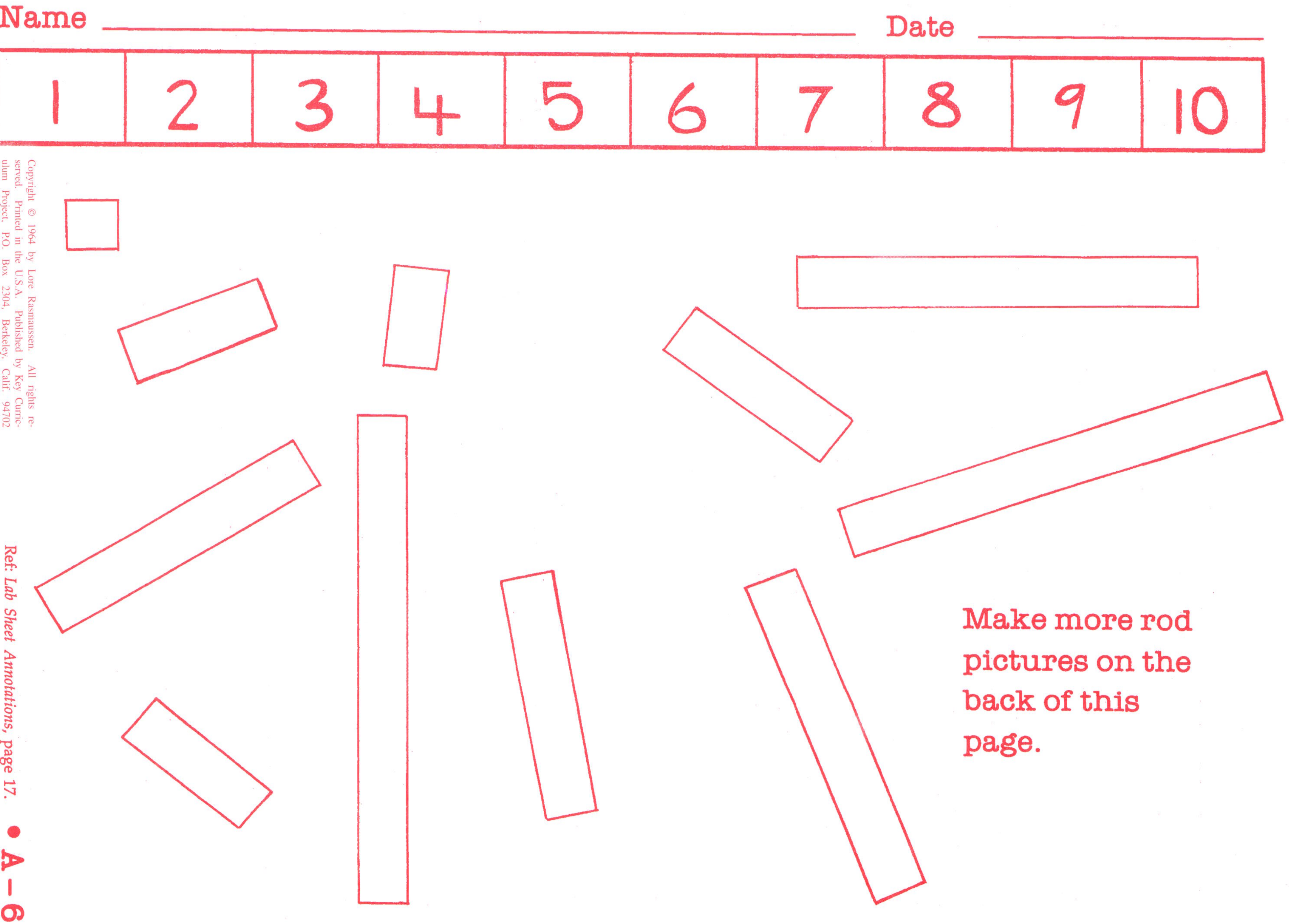

Ref: *Lab Sheet Annotations*, page 17.

Name ____________________ Date ______________

Ref: *Lab Sheet Annotations*, page 17.

Name ______________________ Date ______________

0	1	2	3	4	5	6	7	8	9	10

3	4	5	
0	1		
			8
			10

Ref: *Lab Sheet Annotations*, page 18.

Name ______________________ Date ______________

Follow the Dots

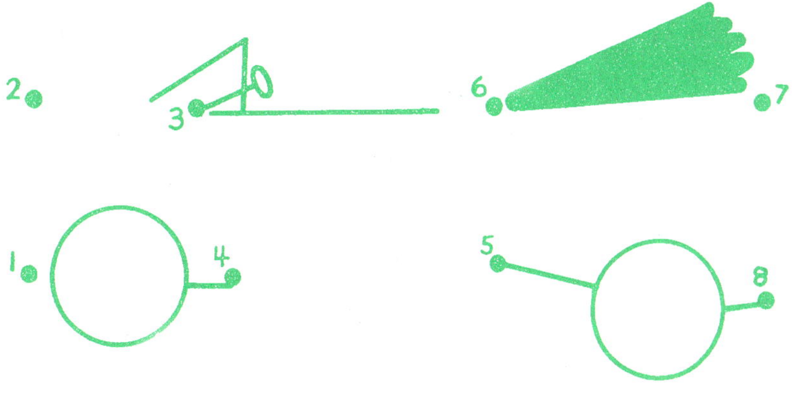

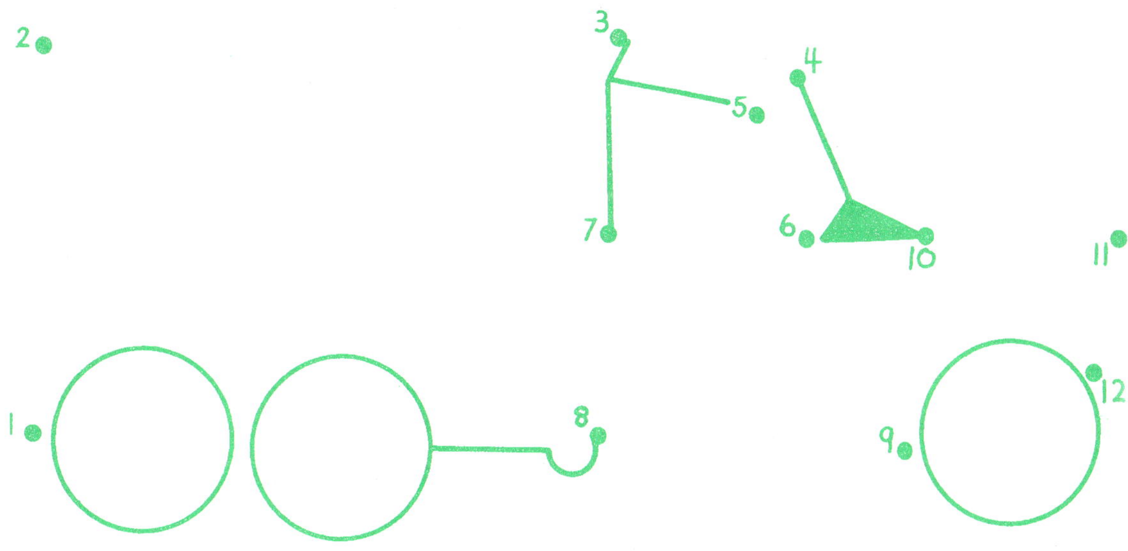

Name ______________________ Date ______________

Follow the Dots

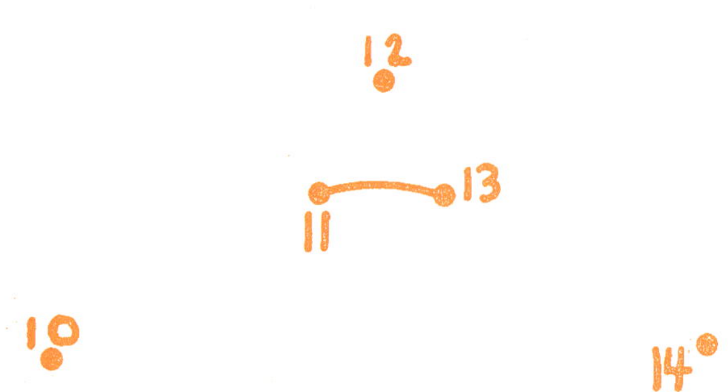

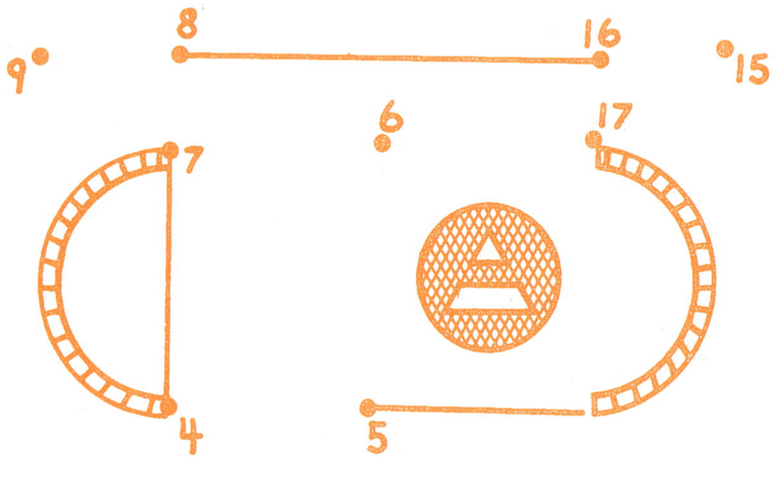

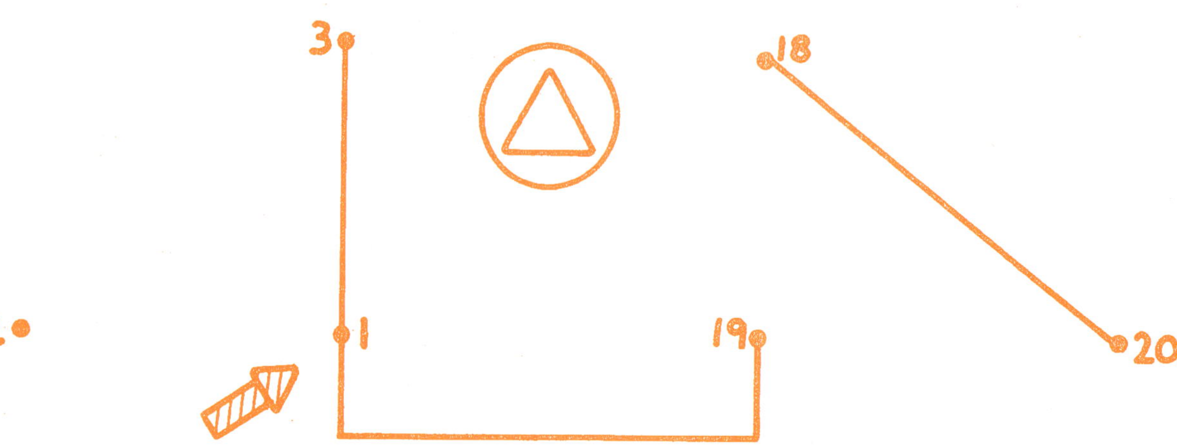

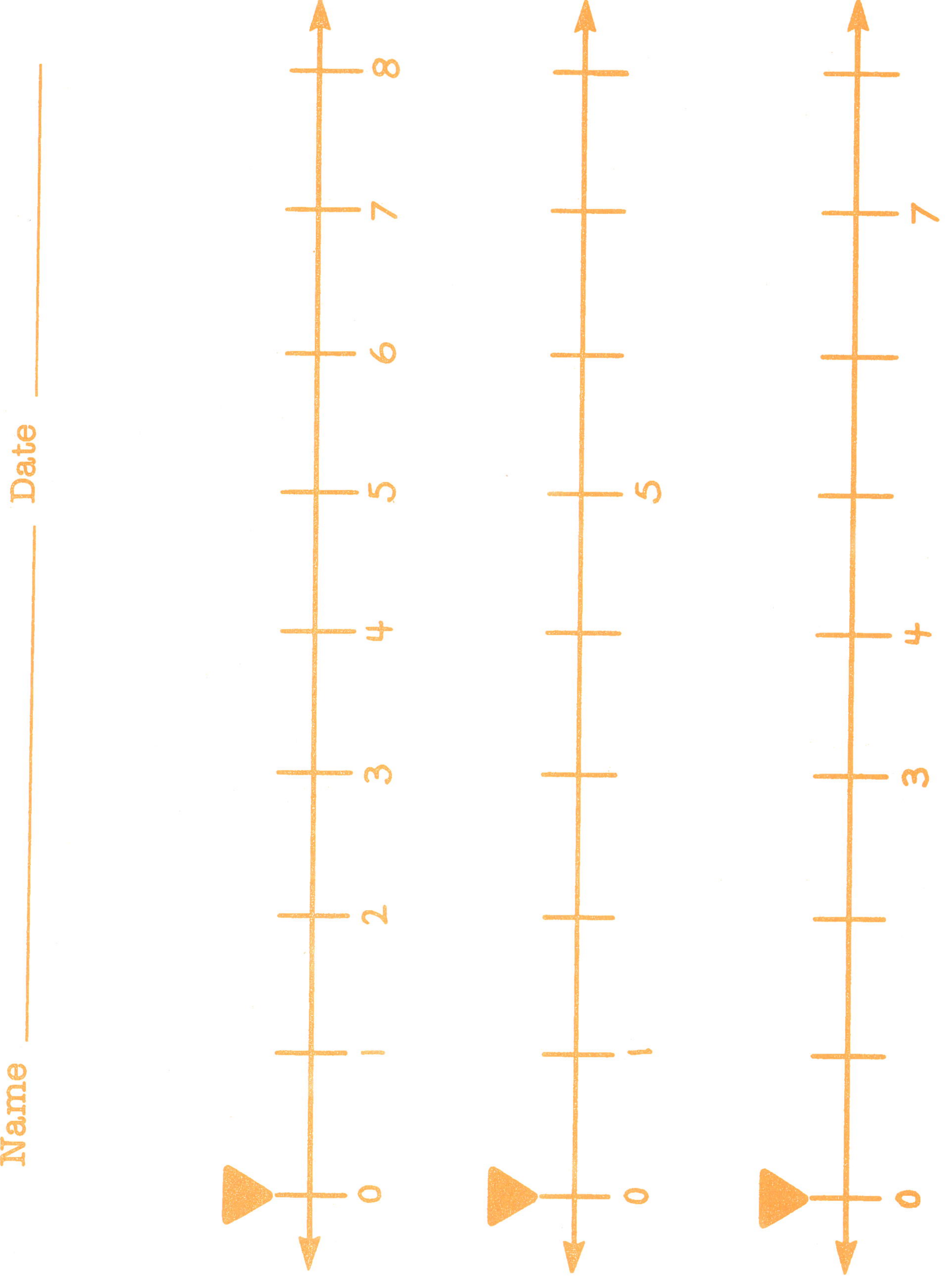

Ref: *Lab Sheet Annotations,* page 19.

Name ______________________ Date ______________

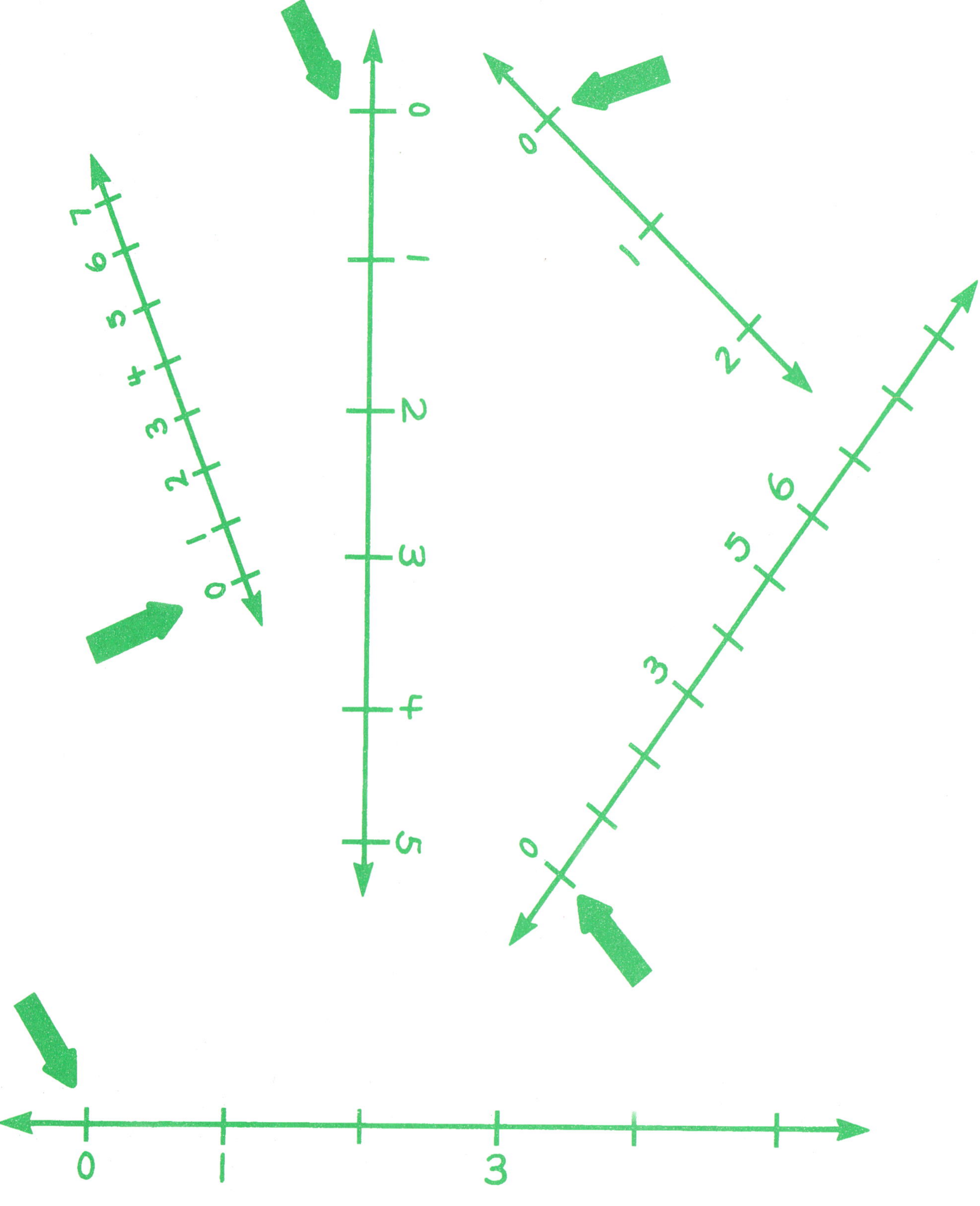

Ref: *Lab Sheet Annotations*, page 19.

Name ________________________ Date ________________

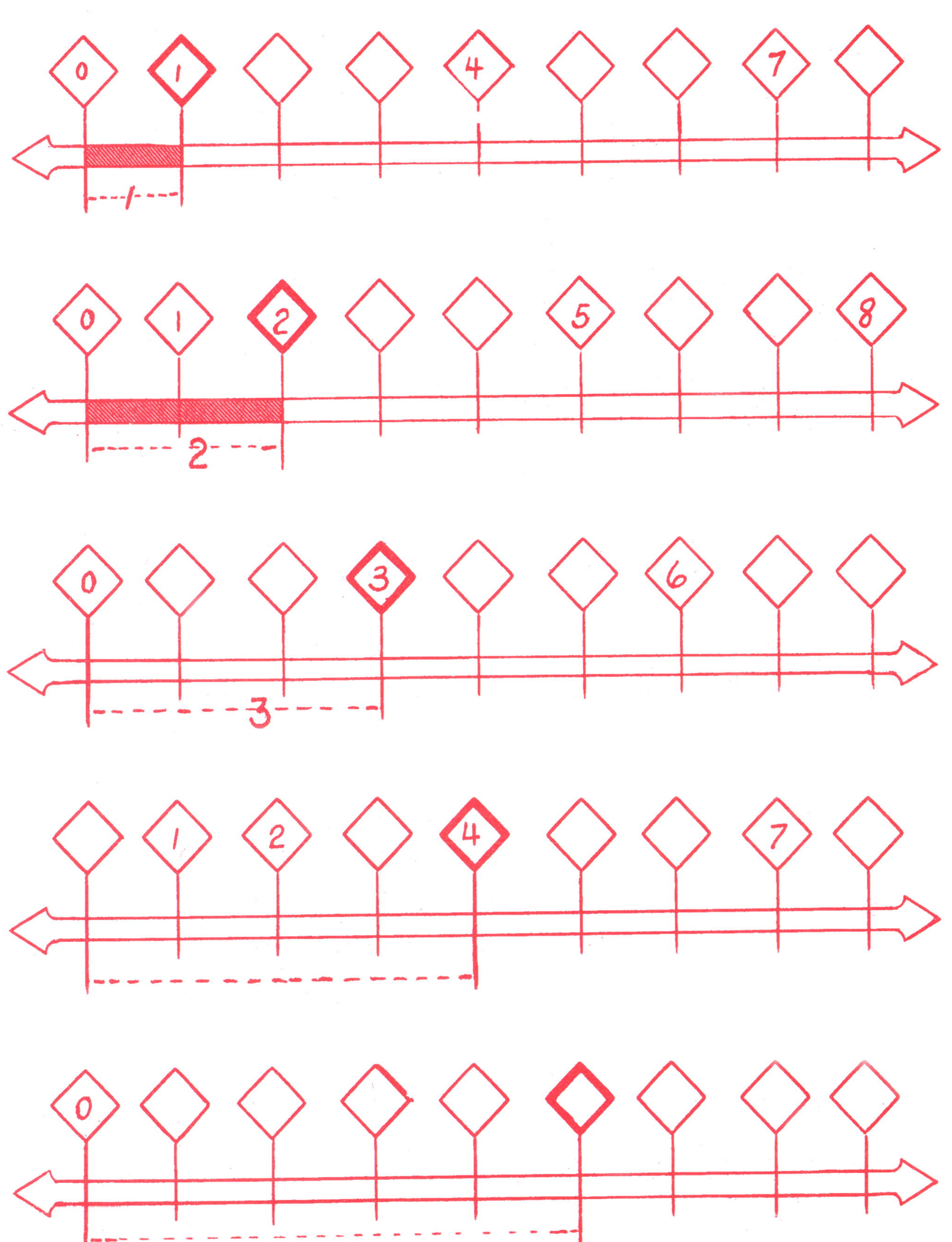

Ref: *Lab Sheet Annotations,* page 20.

Name ______________________ Date ______________

1, 2, 3, ☐, 5

2, 3, 4, ☐, ☐

6, ☐, 8

9, ☐, 11

14, 15, ☐

18, 19, ☐, 21

10, ☐, ☐, 13

Ref: *Lab Sheet Annotations*, page 20.

Name ______________________ Date ______________

Finish the chart.

0	1		3	4			7		
10		12			15				19
			23			26		28	
30		32		34		36		38	
	41		43		45		47		49
50			53			56			59
	61				65				
	71	72	73	74		76	77	78	
80			83		85		87		89
90				94	95	96			99

Ref: *Lab Sheet Annotations*, page 21.

Name ______________________ Date ______________

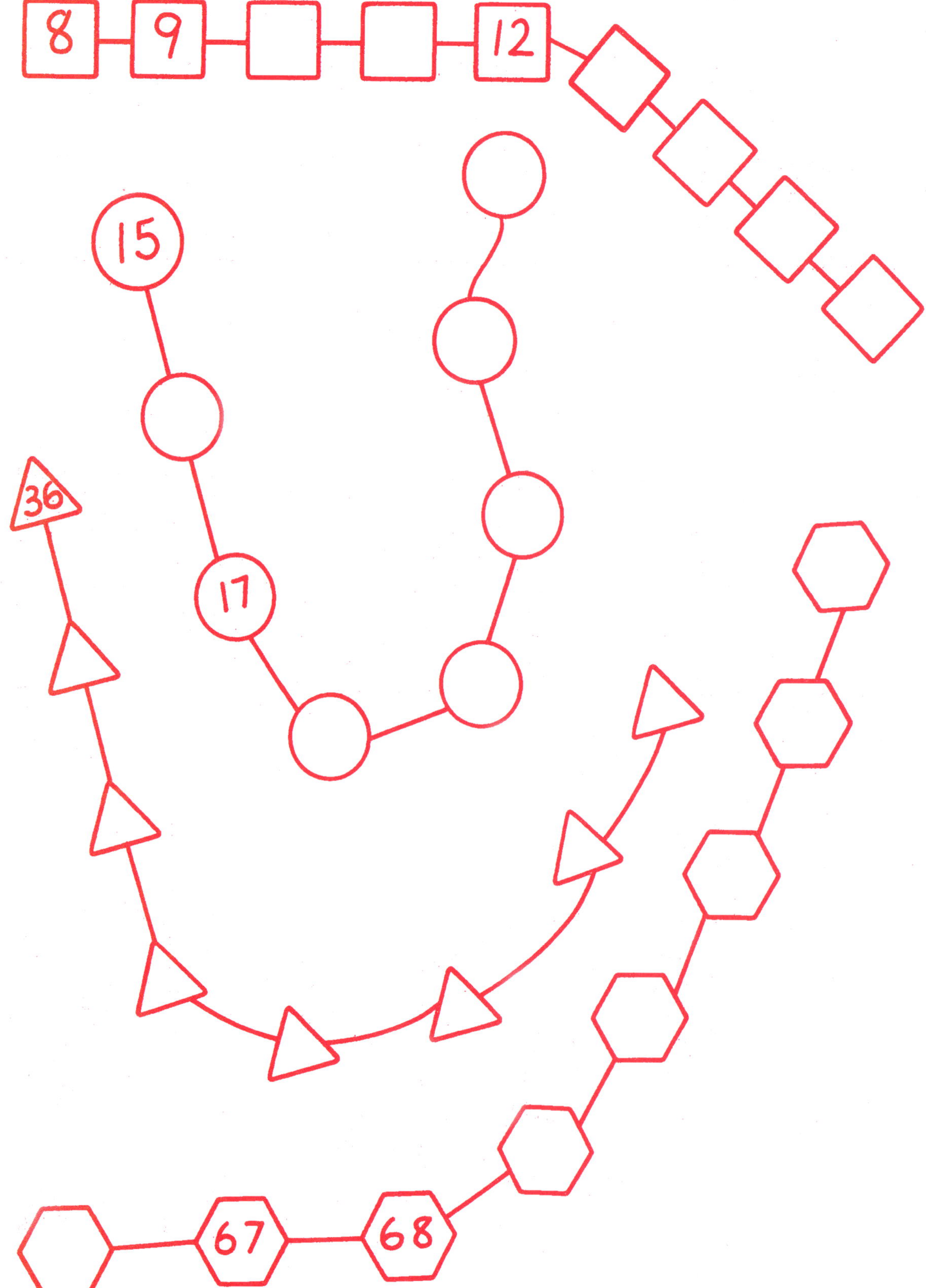

Ref: *Lab Sheet Annotations*, page 22.

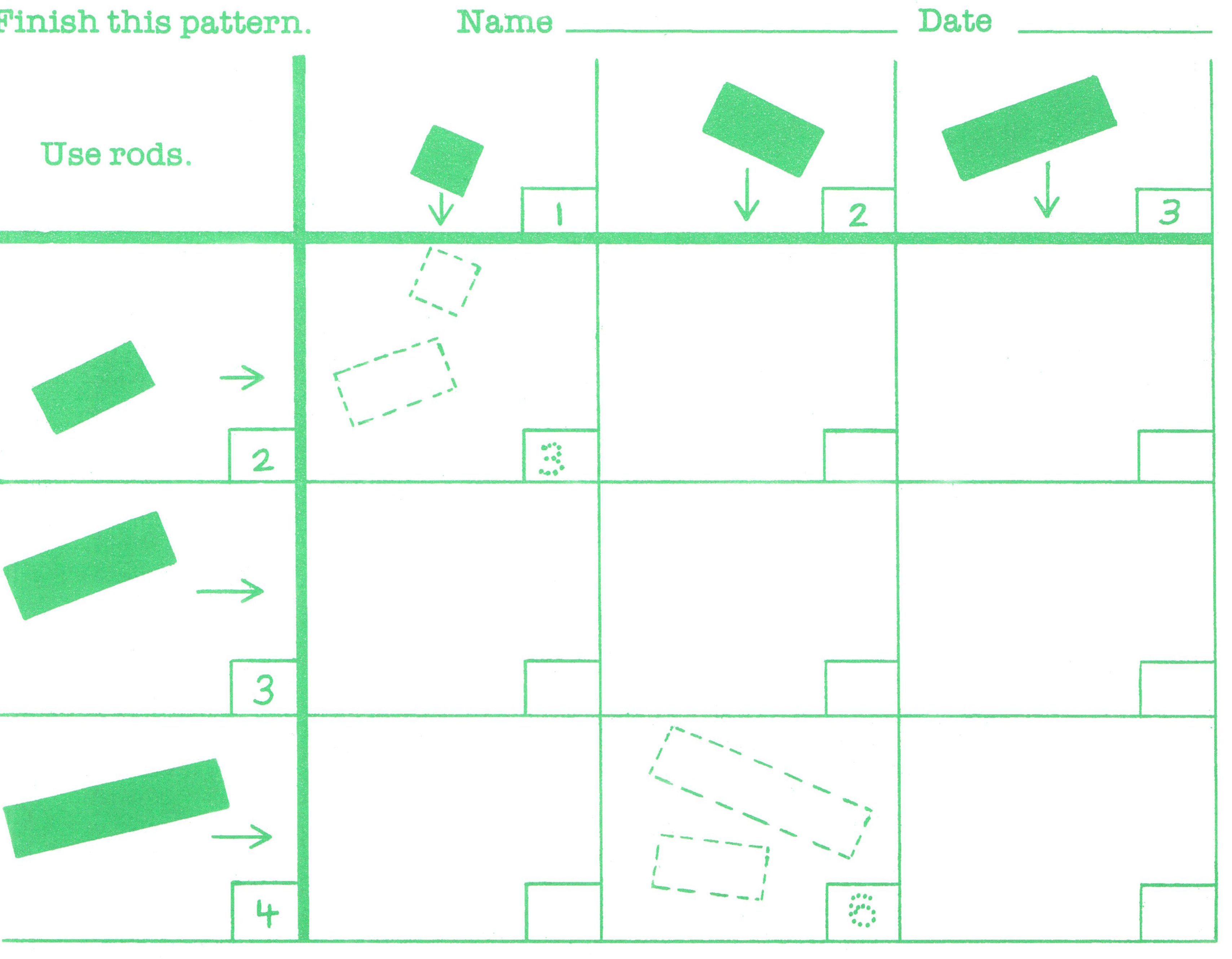

Ref: *Lab Sheet Annotations*, page 23.

Name ______________________ Date ______________

Finish the patterns.

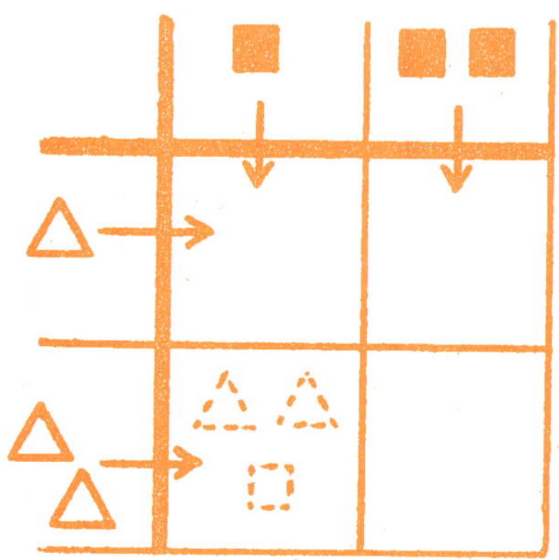

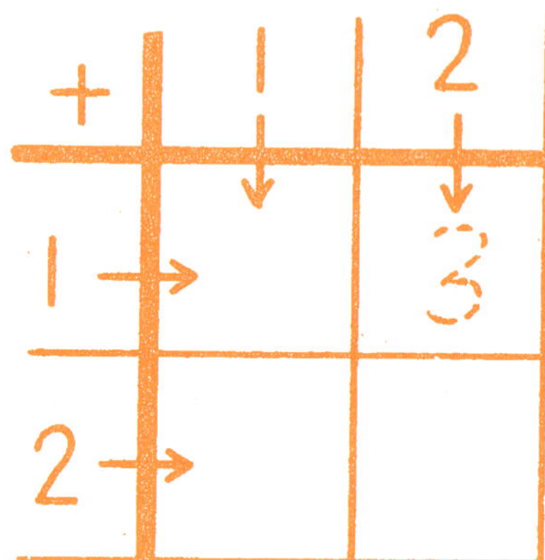

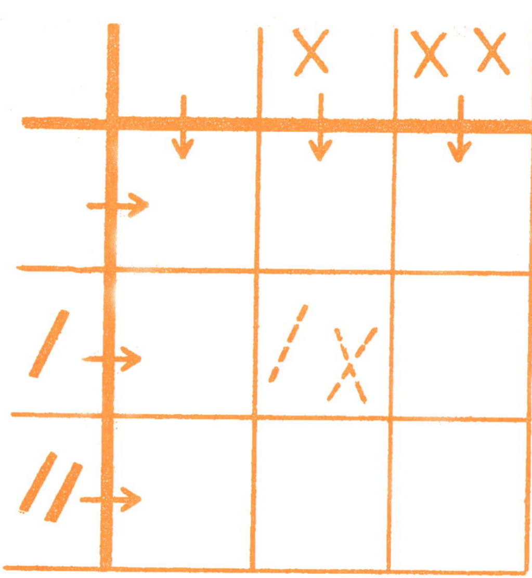

+	0	1	2
0		1	
1			3
2			

Ref: *Lab Sheet Annotations*, page 23.

Name ______________________ Date ______________________

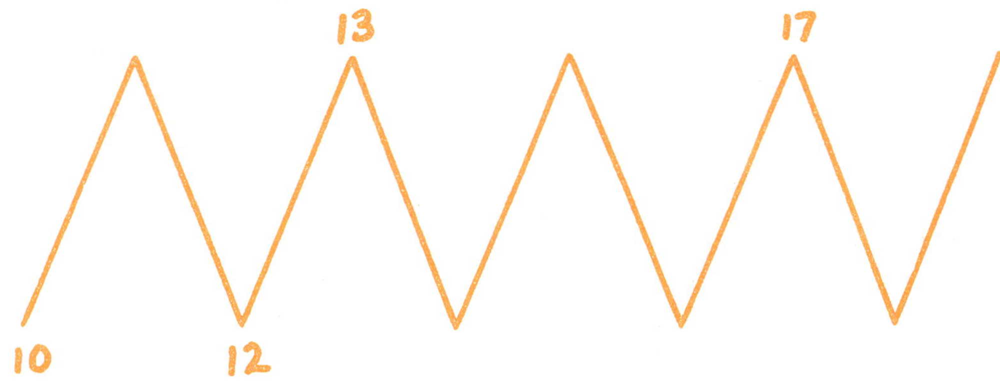

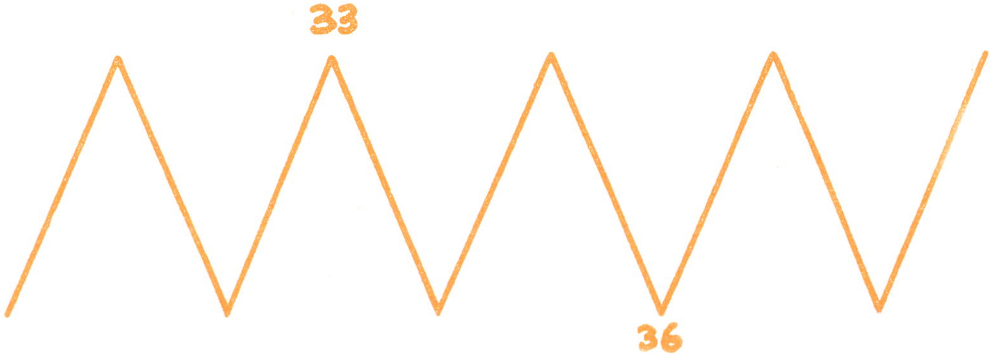

Ref: *Lab Sheet Annotations*, page 24.

Name ______________________ Date ______________________

Find the pattern on each chain and finish it.

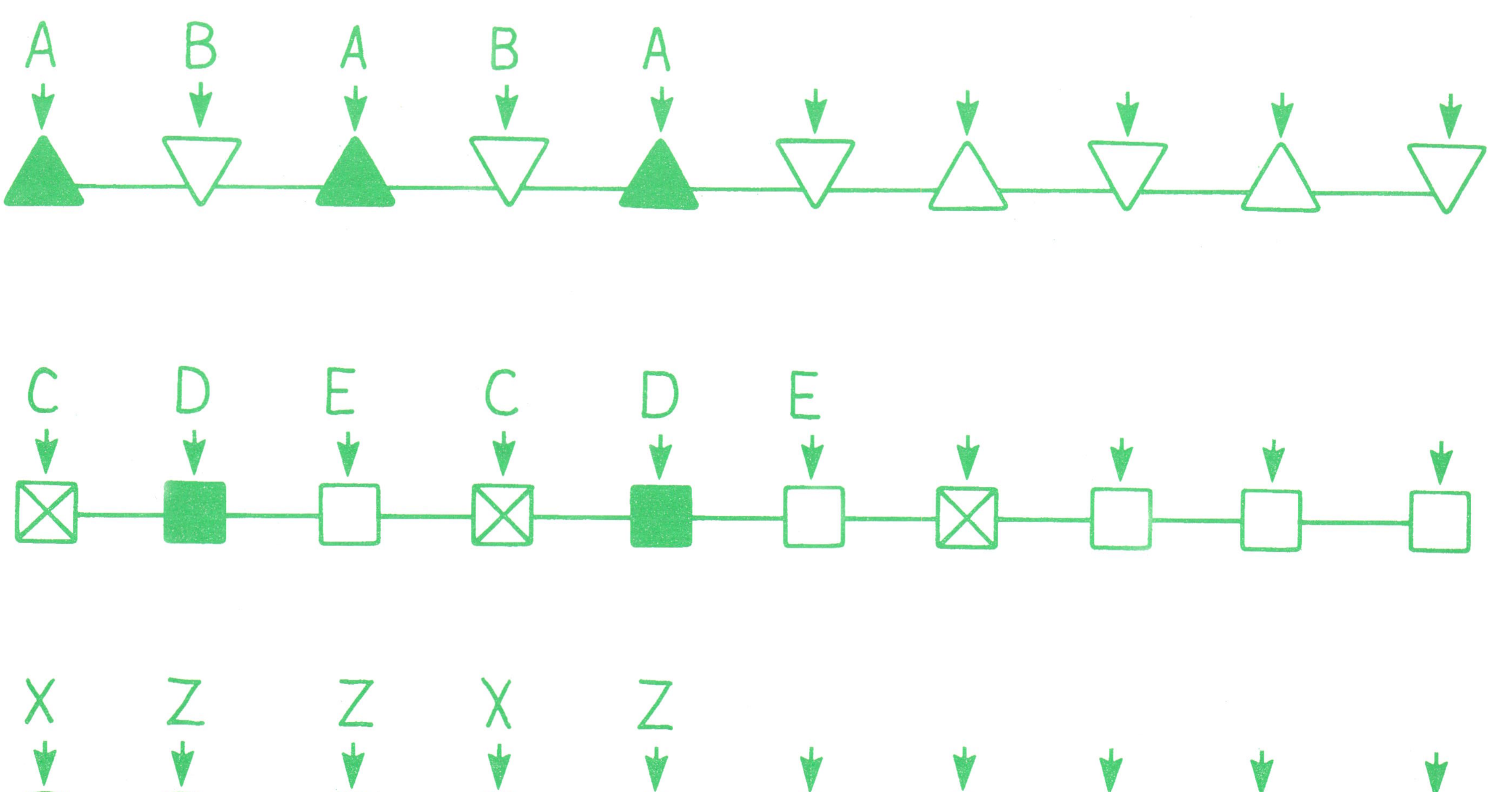

Ref: *Lab Sheet Annotations*, page 24.

Name ______________________ Date ______________________

Find the pattern on this chain and finish it.

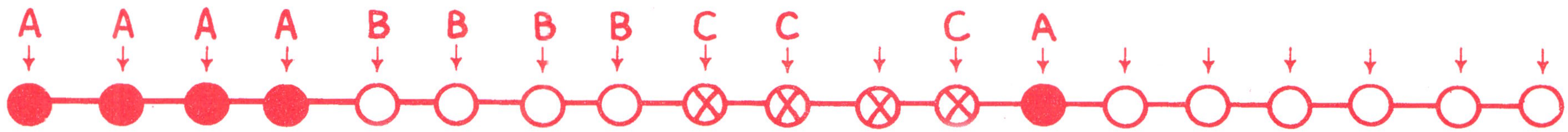

A A A A B B B B C C C A

Color the chain to fit the pattern of the letters.

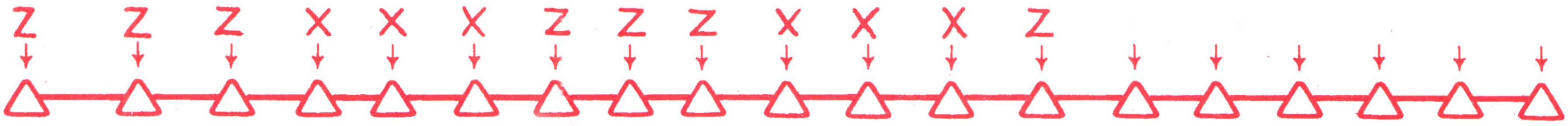

Z Z Z X X X Z Z Z X X X Z

Make up a chain pattern. Draw it here.

Ref: *Lab Sheet Annotations*, page 24.

Name ______________________ Date ______________

Fit the right rod on each part of the rod picture.

How many white rods long is your train? □

How many red rods long is your train? △

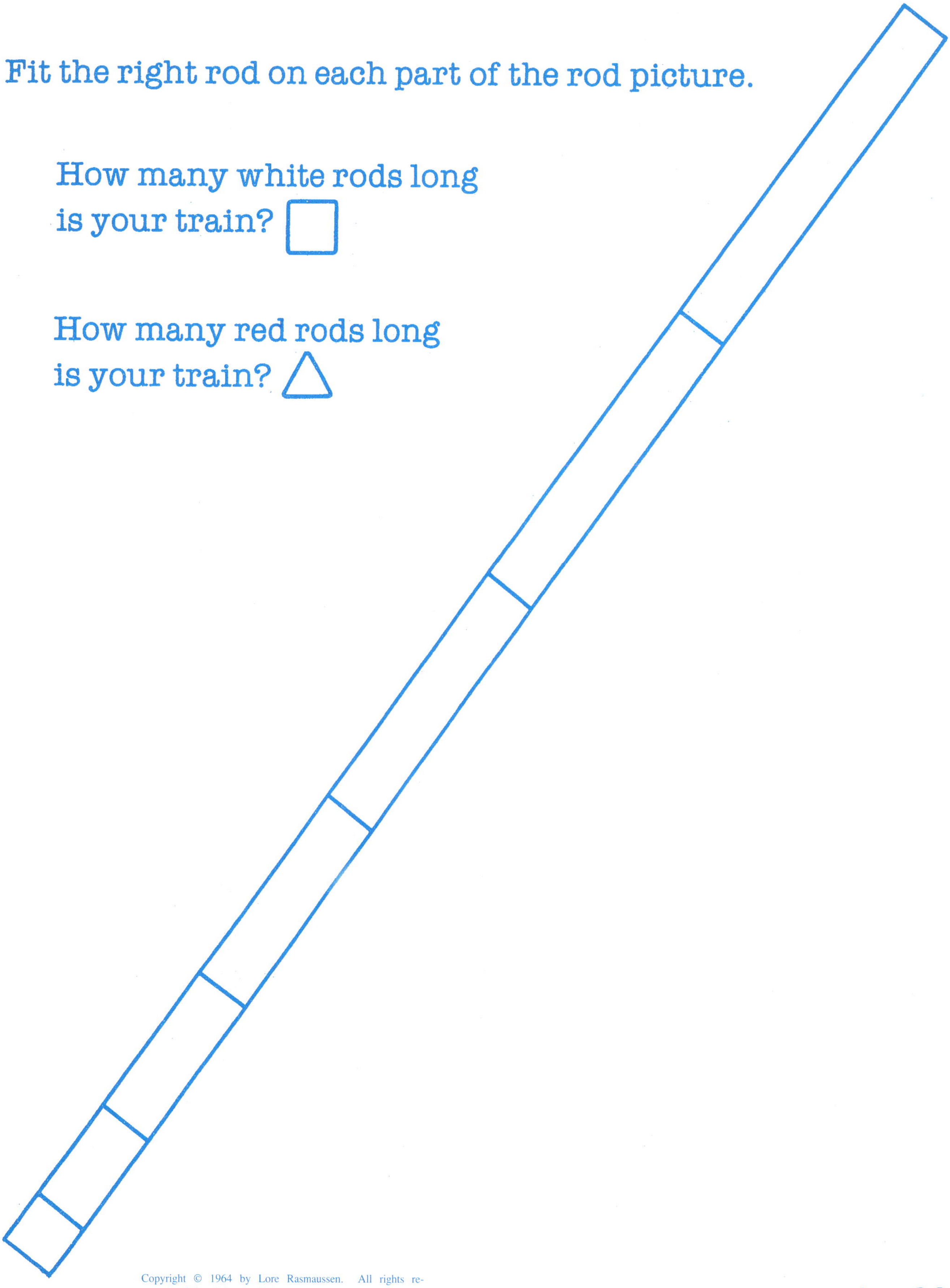

Name ______________________ Date ______________________

Start at 1. Follow the dots.

Color the picture.

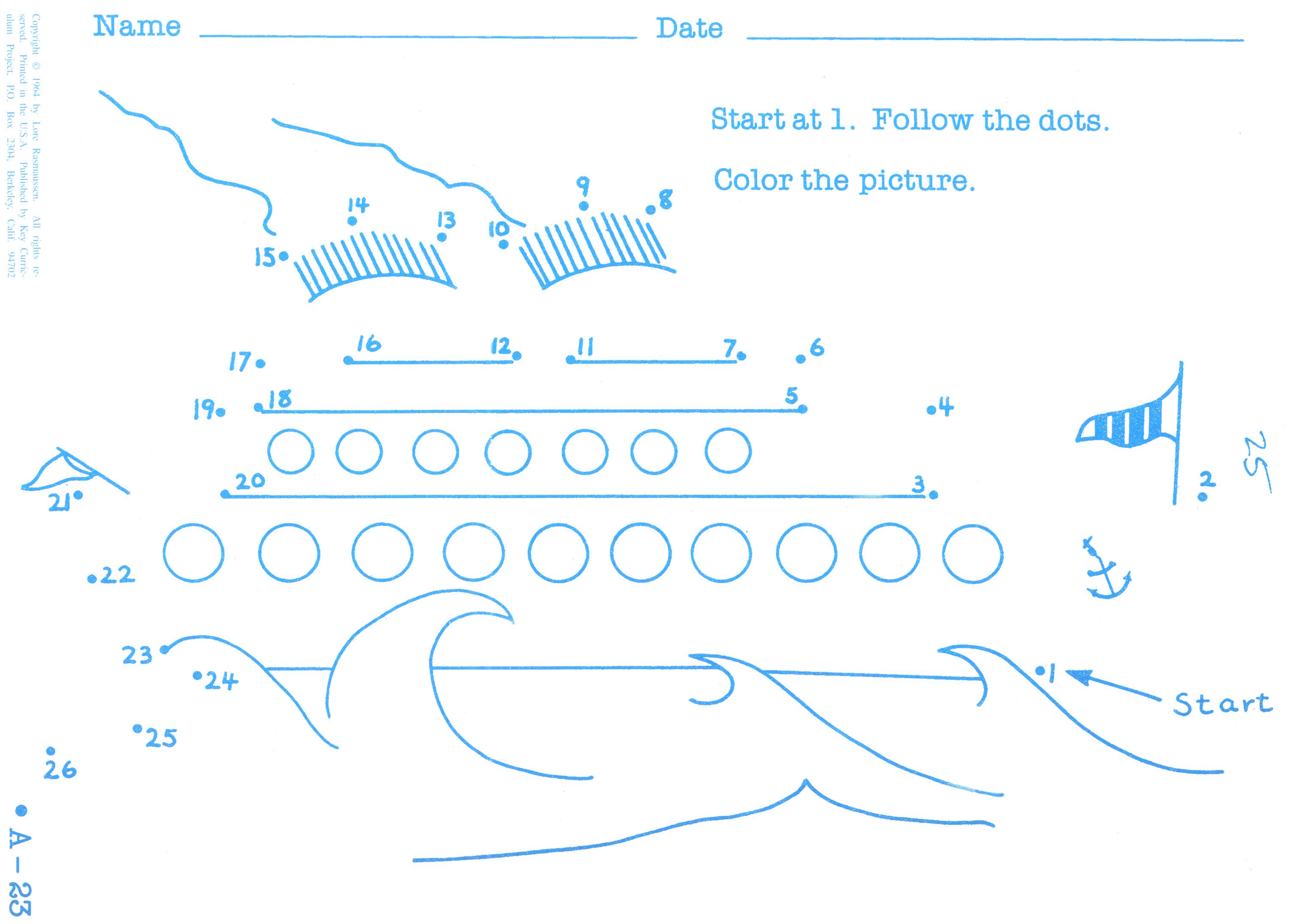

Name ______________________ Date ______________

Cover the rod picture with the correct rods.

How many? ☐

How many? ☐

How many? ☐

How many? ☐

How many? ☐

☐

Start at 0. Jump to 4.

0 1 2 3 4 5

Start at 3. Jump to 4.

0 1 2 3 4 5

Start at 2. Jump to 4.

0 2 4

Name ______________________ Date ______________

4

Use rods.

3 + □

2 + □

1 + □

0 + □

□ + 2

□ + 1

□ + □ + □ + □

□ + 4

Ref: *Lab Sheet Annotations*, pages 37 and 39.

Name ______________________ Date ______________

3 + □

4 + □

2 + □

□ + 1

□ + 3

2 + □ + 2

□ + □ + □ + □ + □

Make up your own.

______________________ ______________________

______________________ ______________________

Ref: *Lab Sheet Annotations*, page 39.

Name ______________________ Date ______________

6 + □

5 + □

4 + □

□ + 3

□ + 2

□ + 1

3 + 3 + □

□ + □ + □ + □ + □ + □ + □

Ref: *Lab Sheet Annotations*, page 39.

Name ______________________ Date ______________

Nine

IX

8 + □

7 + □

6 + □

□ + 3

□ + 2

□ + 1

4 + 4 + □

□ + □ + □ + □ + □ + □ + □ + □ + □

Ref: *Lab Sheet Annotations*, page 39.

Name ____________________ Date ____________________

2 + 1 = □

5 + 2 = □

6 + 3 = □

4 + 4 = □

3 + 3 = □

1 + 1 + 1 + 1 = □

Ref: *Lab Sheet Annotations*, pages 39 and 41.

Name ______________________ Date ______________________

□ = 3 + 2 + 3

□ = 2 + 6

□ = 1 + 7 + 2

□ = 1 + 1

□ = 8 + 2

□ = 5 + 3 + 2

Ref: *Lab Sheet Annotations*, pages 39 and 41.

Name ______________________ Date ______________

$1 + 2 = \square$

$4 + 3 = \square$

$\square = 2 + 4$

$5 + 3 = \square$

$\square = 2 + 2$

Ref: *Lab Sheet Annotations*, pages 39 and 41.

Name ______________________ Date ______________

$1 + 3 = \square$

$2 + 4 = \square$

$\square = 5 + 2$

$\square = 4 + 3$

$6 + 1 = \square$

$7 + 3 = \square$

Ref: *Lab Sheet Annotations*, pages 39 and 41.

Name ______________________ Date ______________

$1 + 1 = \square$

$2 + 2 = \square$

$\square = 3 + 3$

$4 + 4 = \square$

$\square = 5 + 5$

$6 + 6 = \square$

Ref: *Lab Sheet Annotations*, pages 39 and 41.

Name ______________________ Date ______________

$4 + 3 = \square$

$\square = 7 + 1$

$\square = 2 + 8$

$6 + \square = 9$

$4 + 4 = \square$

Ref: *Lab Sheet Annotations,* pages 39 and 41.

Name ______________________ Date ______________

Five

Use rods.

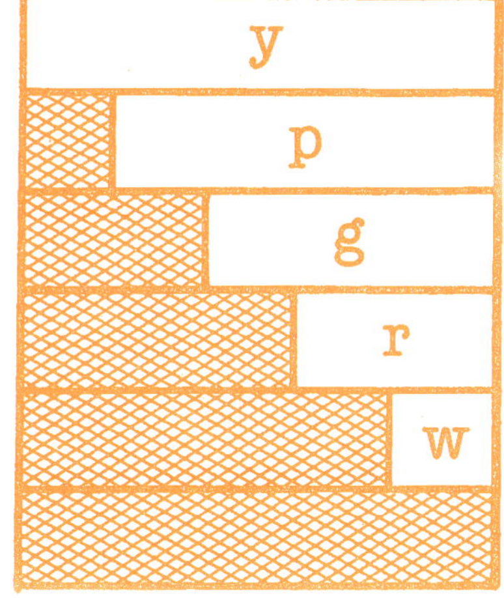

w + ☐ = y

g + ☐ = y

p + ☐ = y

☐ + r = y

Make five.

0 + 5 = 5

1 + 4 =

2 + =

3 + =

4 + =

5 + =

Pairs that make five.

2	4	3	5			1	
3				1	0		2
5	5	5	5	5	5	5	5

Color in the "five" pattern.

+	0	1	2	3	4	5
0					↓	
1	→	→	→	→	5	
2						
3						
4						
5						

Ref: *Lab Sheet Annotations*, page 42.

Name ______________________ Date ______________

Six

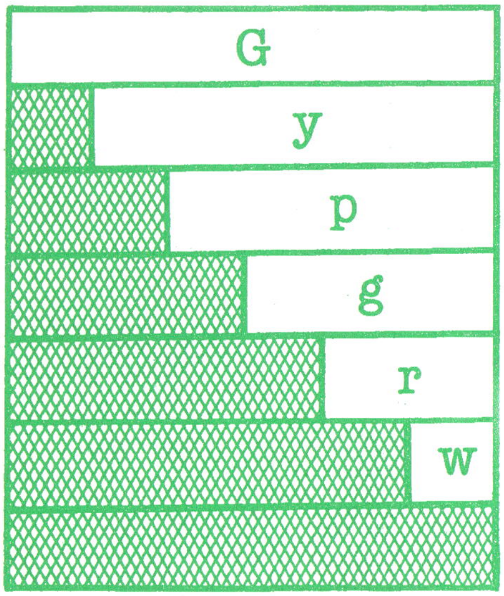

G	
	y
	p
	g
	r
	w

w + ☐ = G

g + ☐ = G

y + ☐ = G

☐ + p = G

☐ + r = G

Make six.

0 + 6 = 6
1 + 5 =
2 +   =
3 +   =
4 +   =
5 +   =
6 +   =

Pairs that make six.

2	5	3			4	6
4	___	___	5	0	___	___
6	6	6	6	6	6	6

Make your own patterns for other numbers.

Color in the "six" pattern.

+	0	1	2	3	4	5	6
0							
1							
2					6		
3							
4							
5							
6							

Ref: *Lab Sheet Annotations*, page 42.

Name ______________________ Date ______________

$4 - 3 = \square$

$5 - 2 = \square$

$7 - 5 = \square$

$3 - 1 = \square$

$8 - 4 = \square$

$10 - 3 = \square$

Ref: *Lab Sheet Annotations*, page 65.

Name ______________________ Date ______________

$\square = 9 - 2$

$\square = 6 - 4$

$\square = 2 - 1$

$\square = 5 - 4$

$\square = 10 - 5$

$\square = 7 - 3$

Ref: *Lab Sheet Annotations*, page 65.

Name ______________________ Date ______________

4 − 3 = ○

⬡ = 7 − 3

○ = 9 − 5

9 − 8 = ⬡

9 − 9 = □

○ = 8 − 8

△ = 7 − 6

3 + 3 − 3 = ○

Ref: *Lab Sheet Annotations*, page 65.

Name ________________________ Date ________________

Which problems are the same?

7 - 4 = △	9 - [2] = 7
10 - 7 = ○	3 = 6 - △
9 - 2 = [7]	□ - 1 = 1
3 - 3 = □	□ = 8 - 5
8 - 5 = ○	2 = 10 - □
9 - 4 = △	△ - 3 = 0
2 - 1 = □	□ = 7 - 4
10 - 2 = ○	10 - △ = 3
6 - 3 = ▽	□ - 4 = 5

Ref: *Lab Sheet Annotations*, pages 65 and 66.

Name ______________________________ Date ____________________

$3 + 7 = \square$

$5 + 2 = \square$

$9 - 5 = \square$

$6 - 3 = \square$

$4 + 2 = \square$

$7 - 6 = \square$

Ref: *Lab Sheet Annotations*, page 84.

Name ______________________ Date ______________

$\square = 9 - 7$

$\square = 3 + 4 + 2$

$\square = 2 - 1$

$\square = 7 + 1 + 1$

$\square = 2 + 6$

$\square = 8 - 6$

Ref: *Lab Sheet Annotations,* page 84.

Name ______________________ Date ______________

$3 + 5 + 1 = \square$

$\square = 2 + 7$

$\square = 9 + 1$

$10 - 1 = \square$

$8 - 4 = \square$

$\square = 2 + 4 + 3$

Ref: *Lab Sheet Annotations*, page 84.

Name ______________________ Date ______________

$3 + 1 + 2 = \square$

$\square = 5 + 5$

$6 - 4 = \square$

$3 + 3 = \square$

$7 + \square = 10$

 Published by Key Curriculum Project, P.O. Box 2304, Berkeley, Calif. 94702

Ref: *Lab Sheet Annotations*, page 84.

Name ______________________ Date ______________

$3 + 3 = \square$

$3 + \square = 6$

$\square = 9 - 4$

$5 + \square = 9$

$2 + 2 = \square$

$\square = 5 + 5$

Ref: *Lab Sheet Annotations*, page 84.

Name ______________________ Date ______________

$2 + 2 = \square$

$3 + 0 = \square$

$1 + 1 = \square$

$3 - 1 = \square$

$4 - 2 = \square$

$2 + 1 = \square$

$3 + 2 = \square$

$2 + \square = 4$

$5 - 3 = \square$

$4 + 3 = \square$

$7 - 3 = \square$

Make up some problems of your own.

Ref: *Lab Sheet Annotations*, page 84

Use rods.

$4 + 2 = \square$

$\square = 2 + 4$

$6 - 2 = \square$

$\square = 6 - 4$

$6 - \square = 2$

$\square - 2 = 4$

$\square - 4 = 2$

$6 - \square = 4$

Name ______________________

Date ____________________

Make up your own problems for this rod picture.

Ref: *Lab Sheet Annotations*, pages 82 and 86.

Name ______________________ Date ______________

Use rods.

$3 + 4 = \square$ $\square = 3 + 4$

$3 + \square = 7$ $\square = 7 - 3$

$\square + 4 = 7$ $\square = 7 - 4$

$7 = 3 + \square$ $7 - \square = 4$

$7 = \square + 4$ $7 - \square = 3$

Ref: *Lab Sheet Annotations*, pages 82 and 86.

Name ______________________ Date ______________

Use rods.

5 + 3 = ☐

8 − ☐ = 3

☐ = 3 + 5

☐ − 3 = 5

8 − 3 = ☐

8 − ☐ = 5

☐ = 8 − 5

☐ − 5 = 3

Make up some problems of your own.

Ref: *Lab Sheet Annotations*, pages 82 and 86.

Name ______________________

Date ______________________

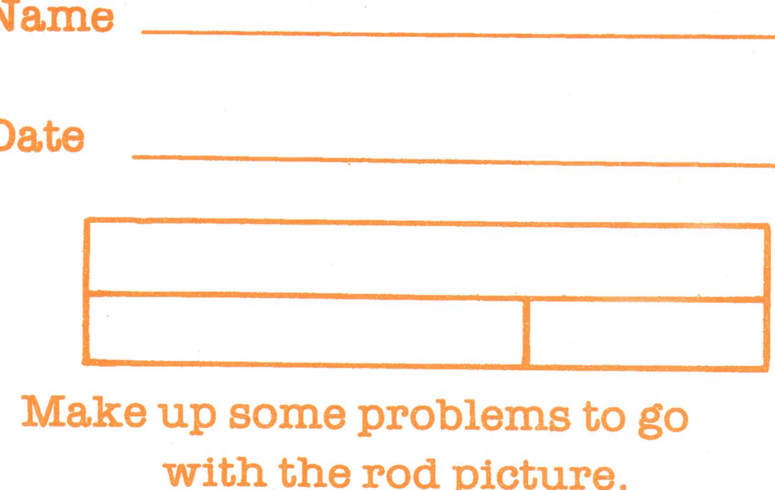

Make up some problems to go with the rod picture.

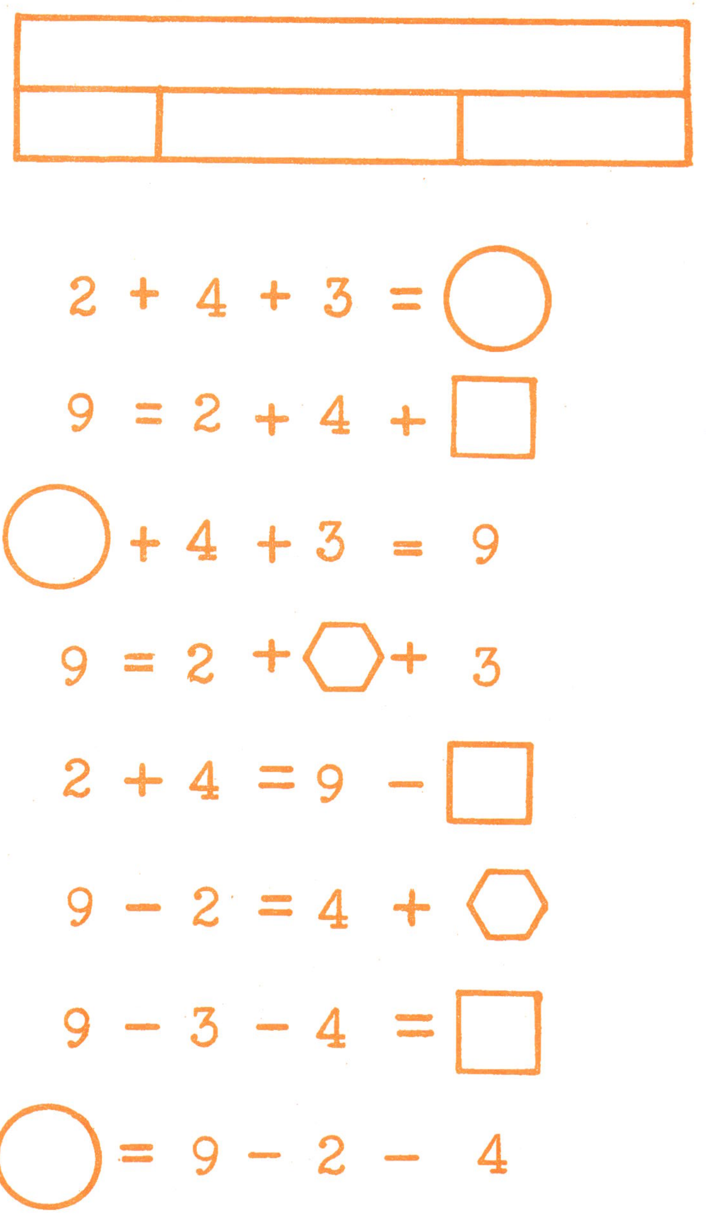

Ref: *Lab Sheet Annotations*, pages 82 and 86.

Use rods. Name ______________________ Date ____________

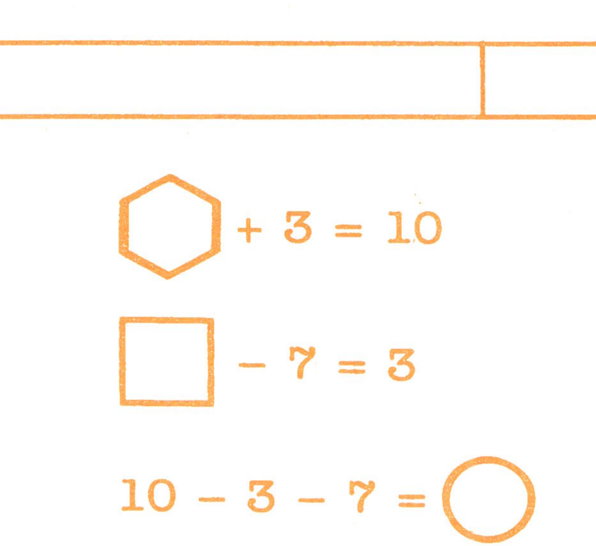

⬡ + 3 = 10

☐ − 7 = 3

10 − 3 − 7 = ◯

Make up some more:

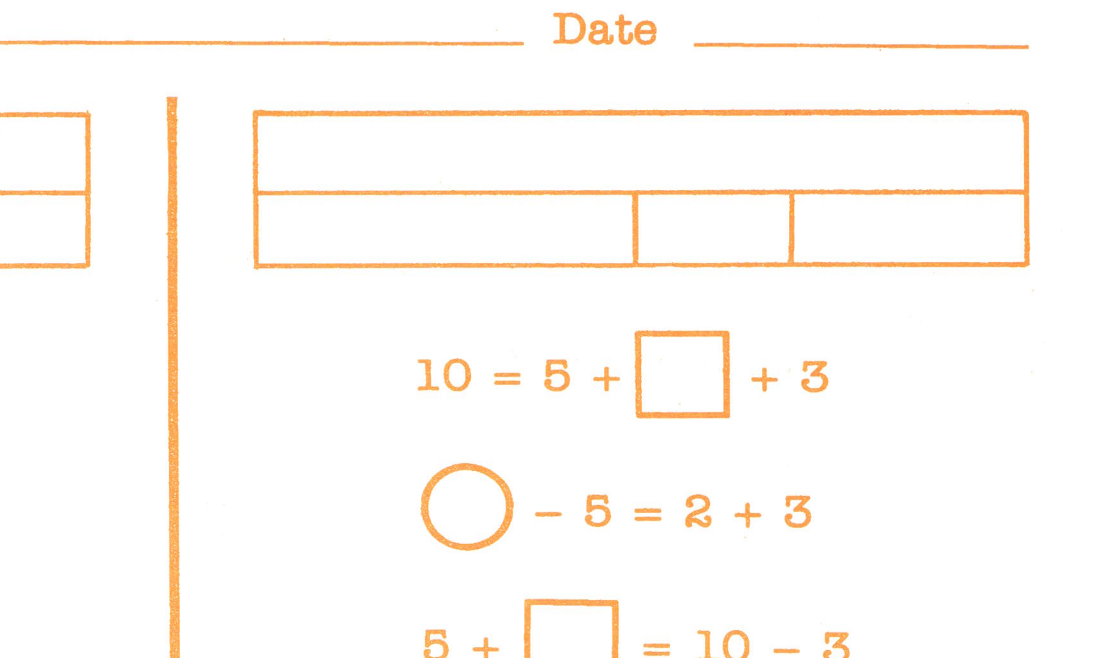

10 = 5 + ☐ + 3

◯ − 5 = 2 + 3

5 + ☐ = 10 − 3

Ref: *Lab Sheet Annotations*, pages 82 and 86.

Name ______________________ Date ______________

$8 = 7 + \square$

$1 + 7 = \square$

$8 - 1 = \square$

$8 - \square = 1$

$8 - \square = 7$

$7 + \square = 8$

$6 - 6 = \square$

$6 - \square = 0$

$0 + 6 = \square$

$0 = 6 - \square$

Ref: *Lab Sheet Annotations,* pages 82 and 86.

Name ______________________ Date ______________________

Make up some problems of your own.

4 + 5 = ○

5 + 4 = ○

5 + □ = 9

4 + ⬡ = 9

9 − 4 = □

9 − 5 = □

9 = 4 + ○

4 = 9 − △

7 − 3 = △

3 + 4 = ○

7 − ⬡ = 4

3 + □ = 7

7 = 4 + □

7 − ○ = 3

Ref: *Lab Sheet Annotations*, pages 82 and 86.

Name Date

This picture shows:

$10 - 3 = \square$ $7 + 3 = \square$

$10 - 7 = \square$ $3 + 7 = \square$

What does this picture show?

$10 - 4 = \square$ $6 + \bigcirc = \square$

$10 - 6 = \square$ $4 + \triangle = \square$

What does this picture show?

Put a loop around nine things.

The picture shows:

$10 - 9 = \square$ $\square + 9 = 10$

$10 - \square = 9$ $9 + \square = 10$

Put a loop around two things.

What does the picture show?

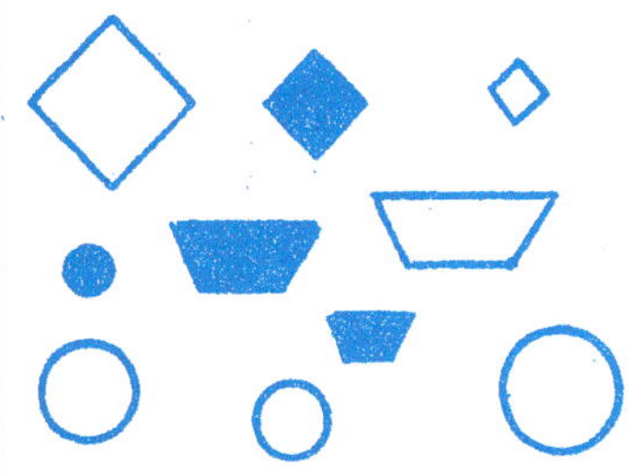

What does the picture show?

Ref: *Lab Sheet Annotations*, pages 82 and 88.

Name Date

$\square = 5 + 3$	$\square = 5 - 3$
$\square = 7 + 4$	$\square = 7 - 4$
$\square = 10 + 7$	$\square = 10 - 7$
$\square = 9 + 2$	$\square = 9 - 2$
$\square = 3 + 3$	$\square = 3 - 3$
$\square = 2 + 1$	$\square = 2 - 1$
$\square = 6 + 3$	$\square = 6 - 3$
$\square = 4 + 3$	$\square = 4 - 3$
$\square = 8 + 5$	$\square = 8 - 5$
$\square = 9 + 4$	$\square = 9 - 4$

Ref: *Lab Sheet Annotations*, page 88.

Name ______________________ Date ______________

+ or −

3 2 = 5

3 2 = 1

7 3 = 4

7 3 = 10

3 3 = 0

3 3 = 6

5 0 = 5

5 0 = 5

---

5 − 5 = □

5 + 3 = ○

□ + 2 = 8

10 − □ = 10

5 + □ + 2 = 8

7 + 3 − 7 = □

5 + 4 − △ = 9

Ref: *Lab Sheet Annotations*, page 88.

Name ______________________ Date ______________

$4 + 4 = \square$

$2 + 2 = \square$

$4 + 1 = \square$

$4 - 1 = \square$

$4 - 4 = \square$

$2 - 2 = \square$

$2 + 1 = \square$

$2 - 1 = \square$

$3 + 3 = \square$

$5 + 5 = \square$

$3 + 1 = \square$

$3 - 1 = \square$

$3 - 3 = \square$

$5 - 5 = \square$

$5 + 1 = \square$

$5 - 1 = \square$

Ref: *Lab Sheet Annotations*, page 88.

Name ______________________ Date ______________

0 1 2 3 4 5 6 7 8 9 10 11 12 13 14 15 16

5 —4→ □

7 —4→ □

□ ←4— 5

□ ←4— 7

□ ←4— 10

4 —○→ 5

4 —○→ 7

4 —4→ □

5 —3→ □

Ref: *Lab Sheet Annotations*, page 89.

Name ______________________ Date ______________

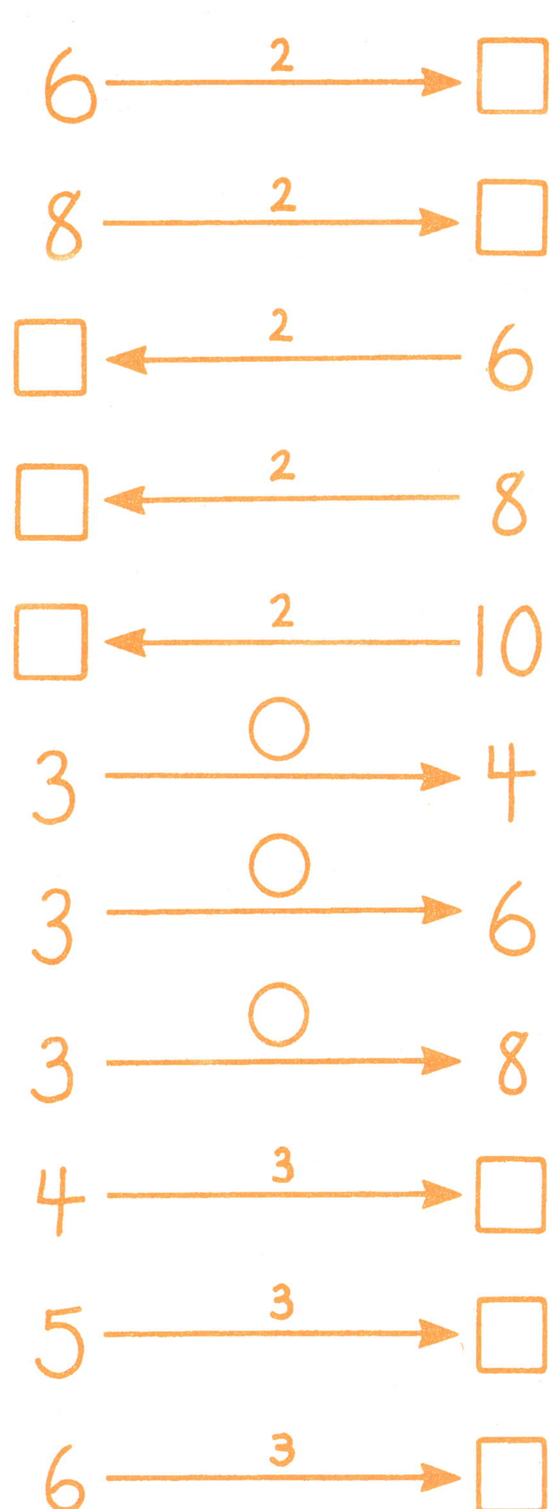

Ref: *Lab Sheet Annotations*, page 89.

Name ______________________ Date ______________________

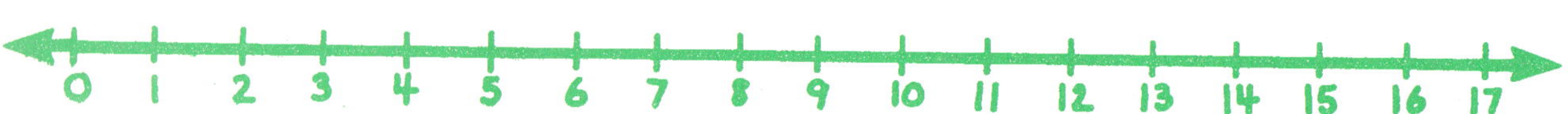

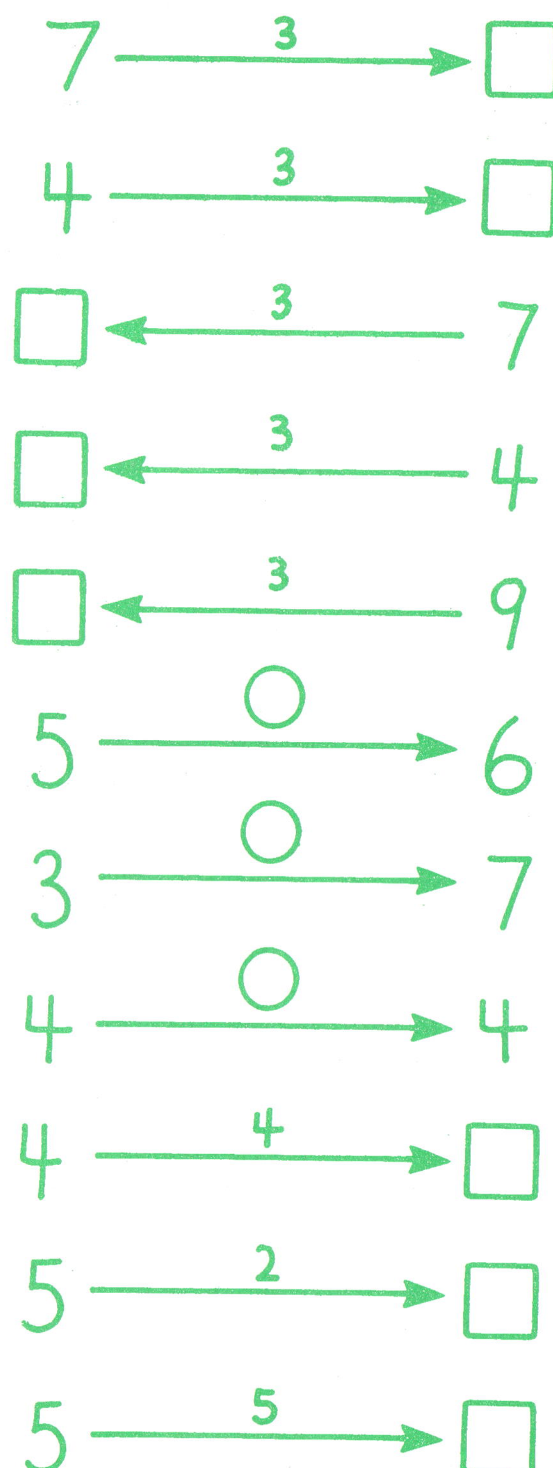

Ref: *Lab Sheet Annotations*, page 89.

Name ______________________ Date ______________

$4 + 5 = \triangle$

$2 + 3 = \bigcirc$

$$\begin{array}{r} 7 \\ +2 \\ \hline \end{array} \qquad \begin{array}{r} 8 \\ -5 \\ \hline \end{array}$$

$\square = 7 - 3$

$\square = 8 + 2$

$$\begin{array}{r} 2 \\ 2 \\ +4 \\ \hline \end{array}$$

$6 + 3 + 1 = \bigcirc$

$\square = 3 + 3 + 3 + 1$

$4 + 3 + 2 = ⬡$

$$\begin{array}{r} 10 \\ -3 \\ \hline \end{array} \qquad \begin{array}{r} 6 \\ -6 \\ \hline \end{array}$$

$\triangle + 5 = 6$

$3 - 3 = \square$

$$\begin{array}{r} 4 \\ +4 \\ \hline \end{array}$$

Name ______________________

Date ____________________

$6 + 3 = \square$

$6 + 4 = \square$

$6 + 5 = \square$

$6 + 6 = \square$

$6 + 7 = \square$

$6 + 8 = \square$

$6 + 9 = \square$

Make up your own problems.

$10 - 3 = \square$

$9 - 3 = \square$

$8 - 3 = \square$

$7 - 3 = \square$

$6 - 3 = \square$

$5 - 3 = \square$

$4 - 3 = \square$

$3 - 3 = \square$

$2 - 3 = \square$

Ref: *Lab Sheet Annotations*, page 91.

$5 + 1 = \square$

$5 + 2 = \square$

$5 + 3 = \square$

$5 + 4 = \square$

$5 + 5 = \square$

$5 + 6 = \square$

$5 + 7 = \square$

Name ______________________

Date ______________

$6 - 1 = \square$

$7 - 2 = \square$

$8 - 3 = \square$

$9 - 4 = \square$

$10 - 5 = \square$

$11 - 6 = \square$

$12 - 7 = \square$

You make up some more problems.

Ref: *Lab Sheet Annotations*, page 91.

Name ______________________ Date ______________

$5 + \square = 6$

$5 + \square = 7$

$5 + \square = 8$

$5 + \square = 9$

$5 + \square = 10$

$5 + \square = 11$

$5 + \square = 12$

Your own problems.

Your own problems.

$6 - \square = 5$

$7 - \square = 5$

$8 - \square = 5$

$9 - \square = 5$

$10 - \square = 5$

$11 - \square = 5$

$12 - \square = 5$

Name ______________________ Date ______________

Use your centimeter rods.

0 1 2 3 4 5 6 7 8 9 10 11 12 13 14 15 16

Start at: Finish at:

0 ——— 1 red hop ——→ 2

0 ——— 2 red hops ——→ 4

0 ——— 3 red hops ——→ ⬡

0 ——— 4 red hops ——→ ⬡

0 ——— 5 red hops ——→ ⬡

0 ——— 1 green hop ——→ ⬡

0 ——— 2 green hops ——→ ⬡

0 ——— 3 green hops ——→ ⬡

0 ——— 4 green hops ——→ ⬡

0 ——— 5 green hops ——→ ⬡

0 ——— 6 green hops ——→ ⬡

Ref: *Lab Sheet Annotations*, page 92.

Name ______________________ Date ______________

☐ = 1

☐ = 1 + 1

☐ = 1 + 1 + 1

☐ = 2

☐ = 2 + 2

☐ = 2 + 2 + 2

☐ = 2 + 2 + 2 + 2

10 =

12 =

☐ = 3

☐ = 3 + 3

☐ = 3 + 3 + 3

12 =

☐ = 4

☐ = 4 + 4

☐ = 4 + 4 + 4

16 =

Ref: *Lab Sheet Annotations,* page 92.

Name ______________________ Date ______________

$3 \times 2 = \square$

$4 \times 2 = \square$

$2 \times 4 = \square$

$2 \times 3 = \square$

$2 + 2 + 2 = \square$

$2 + 2 + 2 + 2 = \square$

$4 + 4 = \square$

$3 + 3 = \square$

Ref: *Lab Sheet Annotations*, pages 108 and 109.

Name ______________________ Date ______________

$2 \times 6 = \square$ $6 + 6 = \square$	$4 \times 4 = \square$ $4+4+4+4 = \square$
$3 \times 3 = \square$ $3+3+3 = \square$	$2 \times 10 = \square$ $10 + 10 = \square$
$3 \times 5 = \square$ $5+5+5 = \square$	$5 \times 3 = \square$ $3+3+3+3+3 = \square$
$2 \times 4 = \square$ $4 + 4 = \square$	$1 \times 1 = \square$ $1 + 0 = \square$

$7 \times 1 = \square$

$1+1+1+1+1+1+1 = \square$

Ref: *Lab Sheet Annotations*, page 109.

Name ______________________ Date ______________

$3 \times 1 = \square$ $1 + 1 + 1 = \square$	$2 + 2 + 2 = \square$ $3 \times 2 = \square$
$4 \times 2 = \square$ $2 + 2 + 2 + 2 = \square$	$3 + 3 = \square$ $2 \times 3 = \square$
$3 \times 4 = \square$ $4 + 4 + 4 = \square$	$5 + 5 + 5 + 5 = \square$ $4 \times 5 = \square$
$2 \times 6 = \square$ $6 + 6 = \square$	$10 + 10 + 10 + 10 = \square$ $4 \times 10 = \square$
$4 \times 3 = \square$ $3 + 3 + 3 + 3 = \square$	$7 + 7 + 7 = \square$ $3 \times 7 = \square$
$5 \times 2 = \square$ $2 + 2 + 2 + 2 + 2 = \square$	$1 + 1 + 1 + 1 + 1 + 1 = \square$ $6 \times 1 = \square$

Ref: *Lab Sheet Annotations*, page 109.

Name ______________________ Date ______________

Which problems are the same?

8 + 8	3 x 5
3 + 3 + 3 + 3 + 3	4 x 2
4 + 4 + 4	2 x 8
5 + 5 + 5	3 x 4
6	5 x 3
2 + 2 + 2 + 2	1 x 6
2 + 2 + 2 + 2 + 2 + 2 + 2	5 x 4
5 + 5 + 5 + 5	7 x 2
4 + 4 + 4 + 4 + 4	4 x 5

Ref: *Lab Sheet Annotations*, page 109.

Name ______________________ Date ______________

Which problems are the same?

4×5	$3 + 3 + 3 + 3 + 3 + 3 + 3$
3×2	$1 + 1 + 1 + 1 + 1$
7×3	$2 + 2 + 2$
2×4	$5 + 5 + 5 + 5$
5×1	$2 + 2 + 2 + 2 + 2 + 2 + 2 + 2$
2×6	$4 + 4$
8×2	$6 + 6$
1×9	$6 + 6 + 6 + 6 + 6 + 6$
6×6	9

Ref: *Lab Sheet Annotations,* page 109.

Name ______________________ Date ______________

$3 \div 5 = \square$ $3 \times 5 = \square$	$2 \times 4 = \square$ $2 \div 4 = \square$
$3 \times 3 = \square$ $3 \div 3 = \square$	$4 \div 3 = \square$ $4 \times 3 = \square$
$2 \times 5 = \square$ $2 \div 5 = \square$	$5 \times 2 = \square$ $5 \div 2 = \square$
$2 \div 2 = \square$ $2 \times 2 = \square$	$3 \times 2 = \square$ $3 \div 2 = \square$
$1 \div 1 = \square$ $1 \times 1 = \square$	$5 \div 1 = \square$ $5 \times 1 = \square$

Ref: *Lab Sheet Annotations*, pages 109 and 110.

Name ______________________ Date ______________

Use rods to help you.

$5 + 5 + 5 = 3 \times \square$

$3 \times 5 = \bigcirc$

$3 + 3 + 3 + 3 + 3 = 5 \times \triangle$

$5 \times 3 = \square$

$3 \times 5 = 5 \times \triangle$

$5 + 5 + 5 = \square + \square + \square + \square + \square$

$3 + 3 + 3 + 3 + 3 = \bigcirc + \bigcirc + \bigcirc$

$2 + 2 + 2 + 2 = \square \times 2$

$4 \times 2 = \bigcirc$

$4 + 4 = \triangle \times 4$

$2 \times 4 = \square$

$2 \times 4 = \square \times 2$

$\square + \square + \square + \square = 2 \times 4$

$4 \times 2 = \bigcirc + \bigcirc$

Ref: *Lab Sheet Annotations*, pages 108, 109 and 110.

Name ______________________ Date ____________

$3 \times 5 = \square$	$5 + 5 + 5 + 5 = \square$
$4 \times 4 = \square$	$2 + 2 = \square$
$2 \times 6 = \square$	$9 + 9 = \square$
$4 \times 3 = \square$	$4 + 4 + 4 + 4 = \square$
$2 \times 2 = \square$	$5 + 5 + 5 = \square$
$5 \times 3 = \square$	$3 + 3 + 3 + 3 = \square$
$2 \times 9 = \square$	$6 + 6 = \square$
$4 \times 5 = \square$	$1 + 0 = \square$
$1 \times 1 = \square$	$3 + 3 + 3 + 3 + 3 = \square$

Ref: *Lab Sheet Annotations*, page 109.

Name ______________________ Date ______________________

Use this picture to help you solve the problems.

$4 + 4 + 4 + 4 = \square$

$4 \times 4 = \square$

$2 \times 8 = \square$

$8 \times 2 = \square$

$1 \times \square = \square$

Make up some problems for this picture.

Ref: *Lab Sheet Annotations*, pages 108, 109 and 110.

Name ______________________ Date ______________

$4 + 4 + 4 = \square$

$3 \times 4 = \square$

$3 + 4 + 5 = \square$

$2 + 3 + 4 = \square$

$3 + 3 + 3 = \square$

$3 \times 3 = \square$

$8 + 6 + 4 = \square$

$6 + 6 + 6 = \square$

$3 \times 6 = \square$

$5 + 7 + 9 = \square$

$7 + 7 + 7 = \square$

$3 \times 7 = \square$

$$\begin{array}{r} 4 \\ 5 \\ +\ 6 \\ \hline \end{array} \qquad \begin{array}{r} 5 \\ 5 \\ +\ 5 \\ \hline \end{array} \qquad \begin{array}{r} 5 \\ \times\ 3 \\ \hline \end{array}$$

Make up some more problems like these:

Ref: *Lab Sheet Annotations*, page 109.

Name ______________________ Date ______________

$3 \times 3 = \square$	$3 \div 3 = \square$
$2 \times 4 = \square$	$2 \div 4 = \square$
$5 \times 3 = \square$	$5 \div 3 = \square$
$4 \times 5 = \square$	$4 \div 5 = \square$
$2 \times 6 = \square$	$2 \div 6 = \square$
$1 \times 1 = \square$	$1 \div 1 = \square$
$3 \times 2 = \square$	$3 \div 2 = \square$
$4 \times 2 = \square$	$4 \div 2 = \square$
$2 \times 7 = \square$	$2 \div 7 = \square$
$2 \times 8 = \square$	$2 \div 8 = \square$

Ref: *Lab Sheet Annotations*, page 110.

Name ________________________________ Date ____________________

$5 \times 3 = \square$

$4 \times 2 = \square$

$6 \times 2 = \square$

$5 + 3 = \square$

$4 + 2 = \square$

$6 + 2 = \square$

$3 \times 3 = \square$

$4 \times 4 = \square$

$5 \times 2 = \square$

$3 + 3 = \square$

$4 + 4 = \square$

$5 + 2 = \square$

Ref: *Lab Sheet Annotations*, page 110.

Name ______________________________ Date ____________________

$3 \times 4 = \square$

$5 + 2 = \square$

$3 + 4 = \square$

$5 \times 2 = \square$

$4 - 3 = \square$

$2 \times 5 = \square$

$4 \times 3 = \square$

$5 - 2 = \square$

$2 \times 4 = \square$

$4 \times 2 = \square$

Name ______________________ Date ______________

$5 - \square = 3$

$4 - \square = 1$

$\square - 2 = 3$

$\square - 3 = 1$

$\square \times 4 = 12$

$2 \times \square = 8$

$4 \times \square = 12$

$\square \times 2 = 8$

$\begin{array}{r} 5 \\ +6 \\ \hline \end{array}$ $\begin{array}{r} 10 \\ +11 \\ \hline \end{array}$ $\begin{array}{r} 4 \\ +5 \\ \hline \end{array}$ $\begin{array}{r} 6 \\ +7 \\ \hline \end{array}$ $\begin{array}{r} 3 \\ +4 \\ \hline \end{array}$

$\begin{array}{r} 15 \\ +6 \\ \hline \end{array}$ $\begin{array}{r} 20 \\ +11 \\ \hline \end{array}$ $\begin{array}{r} 14 \\ +5 \\ \hline \end{array}$ $\begin{array}{r} 16 \\ +7 \\ \hline \end{array}$ $\begin{array}{r} 13 \\ +4 \\ \hline \end{array}$

Name ______________________ Date ______________

$3 + 4 = \square$

$2 \times 3 = \square$

$7 + 7 = \square$

$\square = 2 \times 4$

$\square = 9 - 7$

$\square = 4 \times 2$

$8 + 0 = \square$

$3 \times 2 = \square$

$\square = 3 \times 5$

$9 - 4 = \square$

$12 - 10 = \square$

$4 + 5 = \square$

$12 - 2 = \square$

$5 + \square = 9$

$10 + \square = 12$

$7 + 2 + 3 = \square$

Make up your own problems.

$\square = 8 - 0$

$8 - 8 = \square$

Name ______________________ Date ______________

Find the TENS and ADD.

2 + 6 + 8 + 4 = ◯

5 + 8 + 7 + 5 + 2 + 3 = ⬡

1 + 3 + 9 + 7 = ◯

⬡ = 8 + 8 + 8 + 2 + 2 + 2

1 + 4 + 10 + 5 = ◯

◯ = 3 + 7 + 8

4 + 6 + 4 + 2 + 8 = ⬡

◯ = 10 + 10 + 4 + 10 + 6

1 + 2 + 3 + 4 + 5 + 5 + 6 + 7 + 8 + 9 = ⬡

◯ = (5 x 10) + (3 x 10)

Name ______________________ Date ______________

Draw a line to the big 10 when the answer is 10.

2 + 7

13 − 3

4 + 6

1 + 3 + 5

15 − 5

2 × 5

17 − 10

10 − 0

10 × 1

4 + 10 − 4

0 × 10

0 + 10

1 + 2 + 3 + 4

Ref: *Lab Sheet Annotations*, page 135.

Name ______________________________ Date ____________________

Draw a line to the big 9 when the answer is 9.

3x3

7+1

1+8

6+3

5x4

11-2

5+3

9

5+8-4

9x1

0+9

1+9

9x0

2+2+2+2

3+3+3

13-2-2

7-2

15-7

19-9

17-7

14-5

19-10

Ref: *Lab Sheet Annotations*, page 135.

Name ______________________ Date ______________

Draw a line to the big [12] when the answer is 12.

10+2

2+2+2+2+2

3x4

2x10

12x0

1x21

1x12

12

1x11

16-4

6x2

6x6

3+3+3+3

(2x3)+(3x2)

1+14+1-3

12x1

12+0+0-0

21+0

4+4+4

12+1

(2x5)+1

Ref: *Lab Sheet Annotations,* page 135.

Name ______________________ Date ______________

Fill in the frames with names for 100.

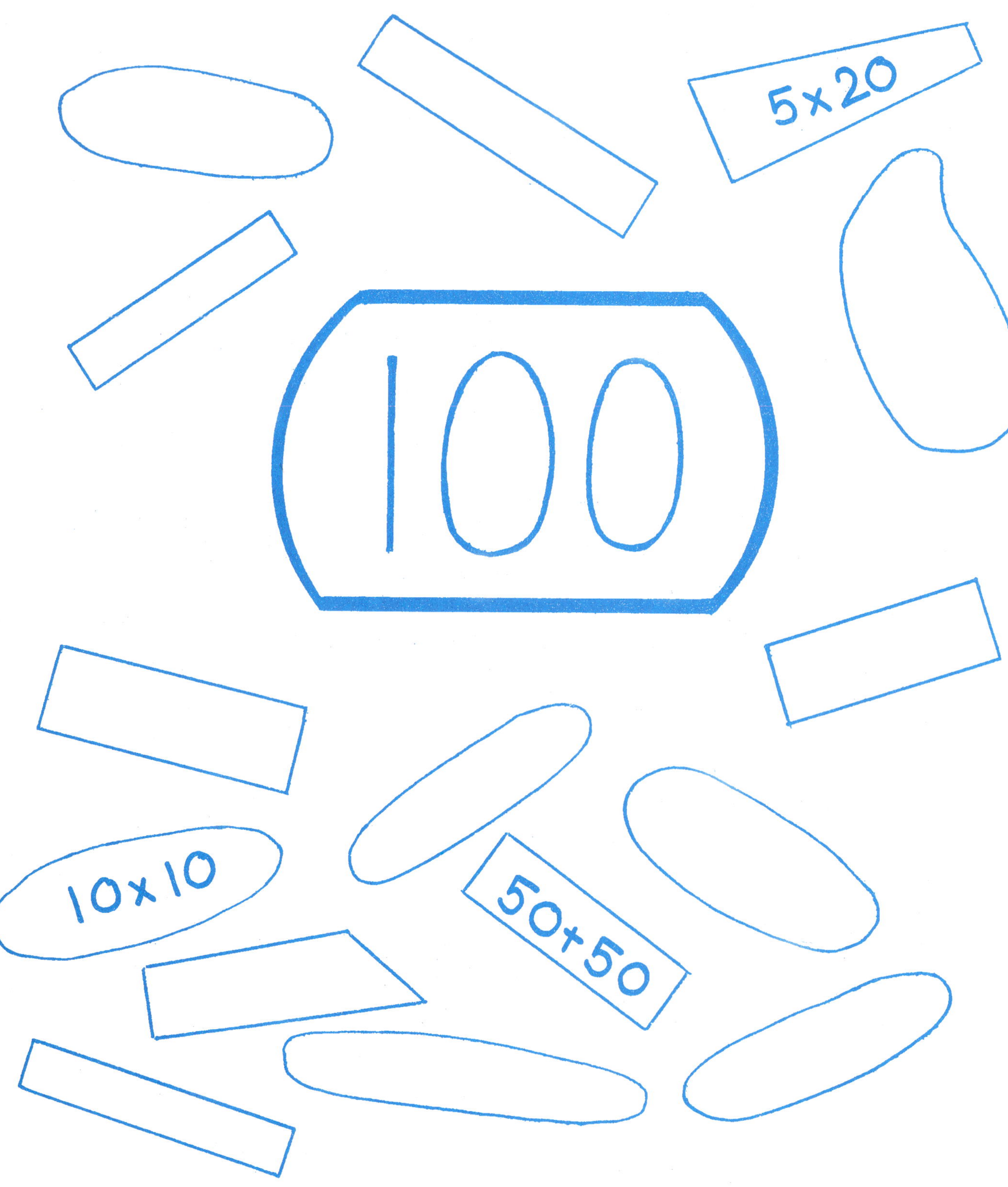

Ref: *Lab Sheet Annotations*, page 135.

Name ______________________ Date ______________

$\frac{1}{2}$

Find a rod that is <u>one-half</u>
<u>as long</u> as each rod picture.
Draw it in the picture.

$\frac{1}{2}$ of 4 = (2)

$\frac{1}{2}$ of 2 = △

5 = □ of 10

6 = □ of ○

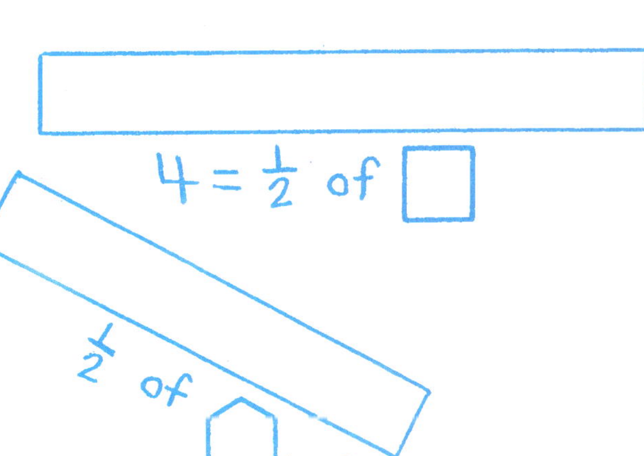

$\frac{1}{3}$

Do the same for <u>one-third</u>.

1 = $\frac{1}{3}$ of ○

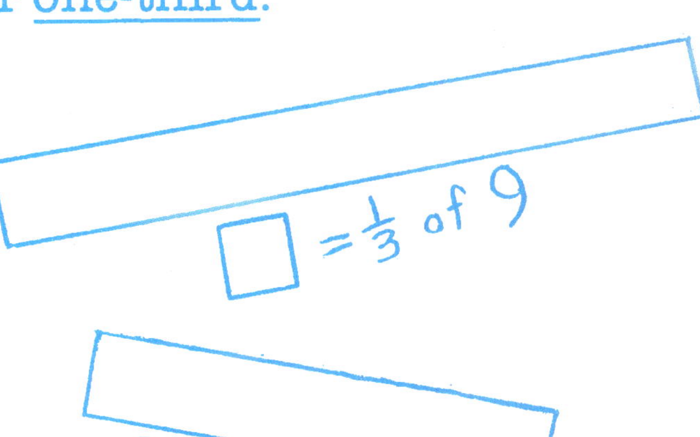

Ref: *Lab Sheet Annotations*, page 142.

Name ______________________ Date ______________

Put a loop around the name for the white part in each picture.

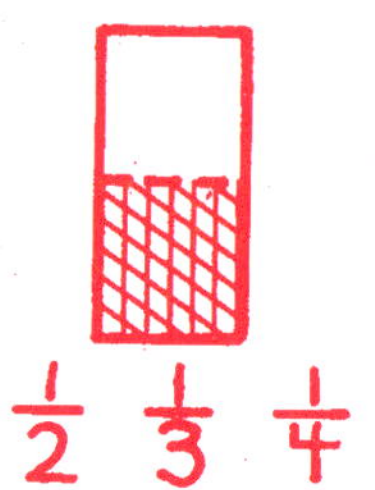

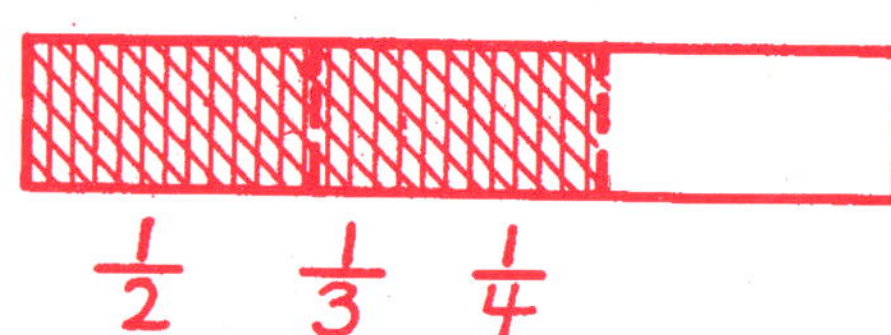

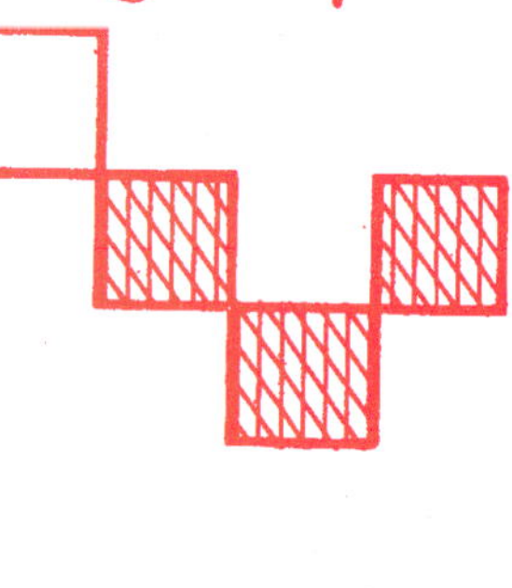

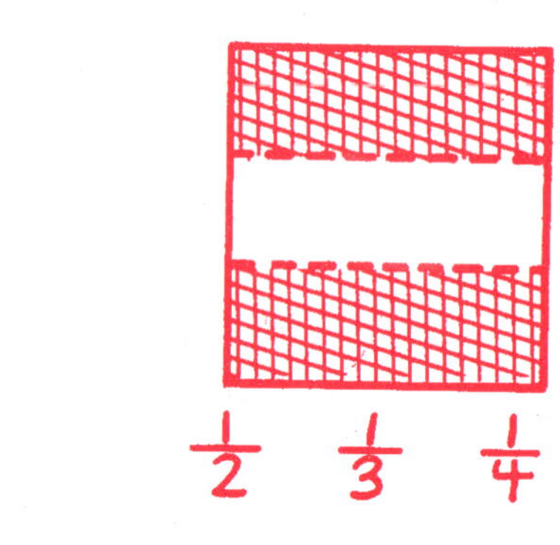

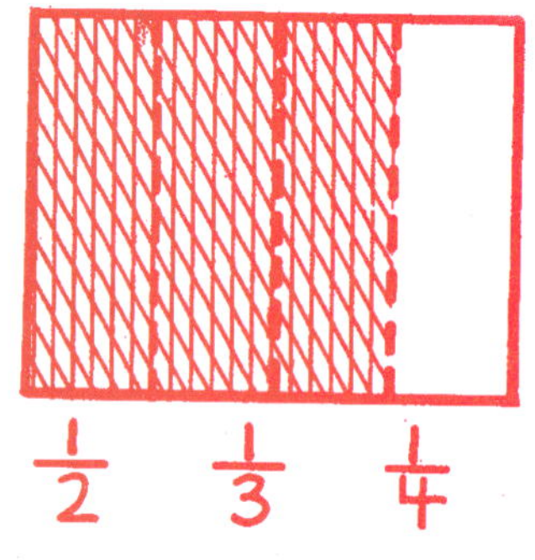

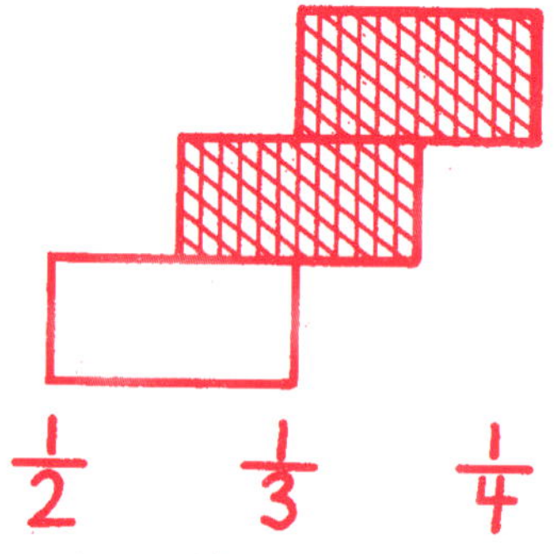

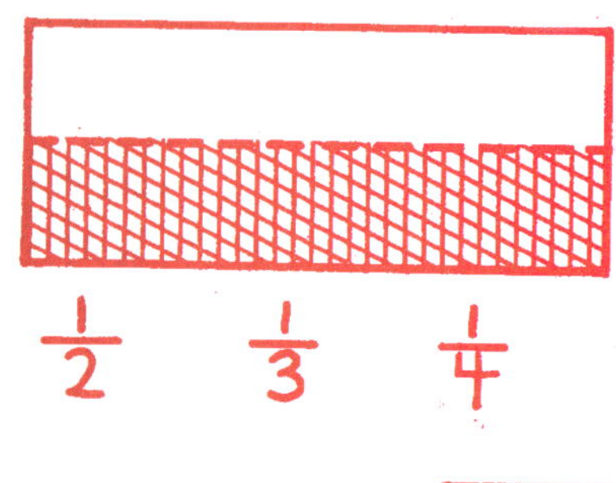

$\frac{1}{2}$ $\frac{1}{3}$ $\frac{1}{4}$

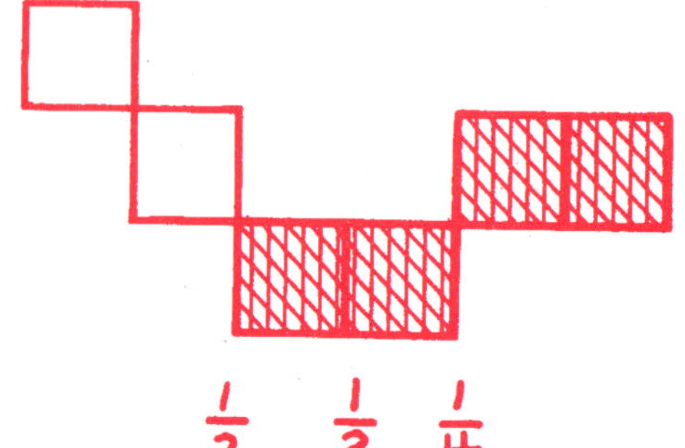

Ref: *Lab Sheet Annotations*, pages 142 and 143.

Name ______________________ Date ______________

WHAT PART IS SHADED IN?

$\frac{1}{2}$ $\frac{1}{3}$ $\frac{1}{4}$ $\frac{1}{5}$ $\frac{1}{6}$ $\frac{1}{7}$ $\frac{1}{8}$ $\frac{1}{9}$ $\frac{1}{10}$ $\frac{1}{11}$ $\frac{1}{12}$ $\frac{1}{13}$ $\frac{1}{14}$ $\frac{1}{15}$ $\frac{1}{16}$

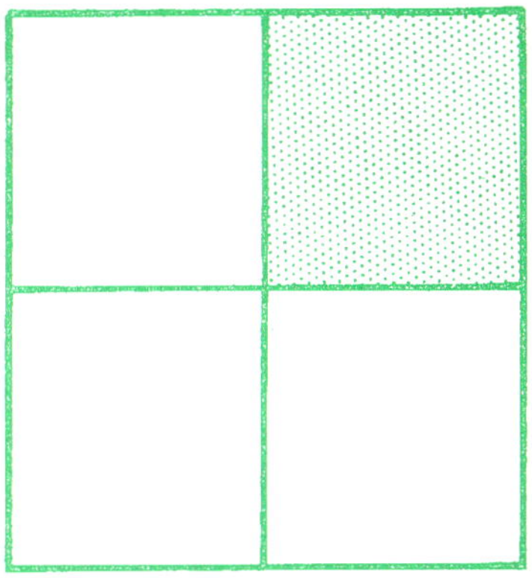

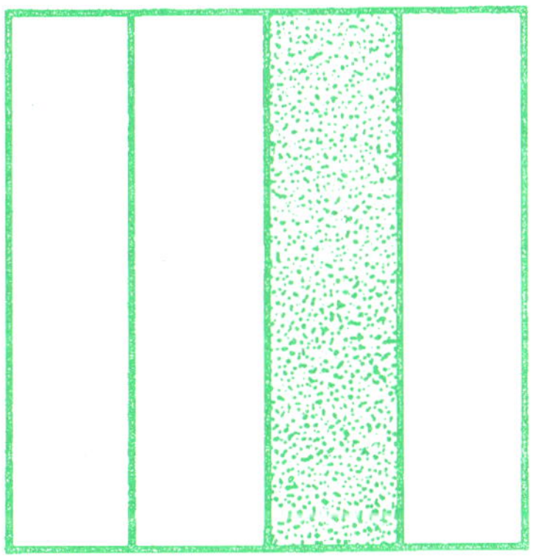

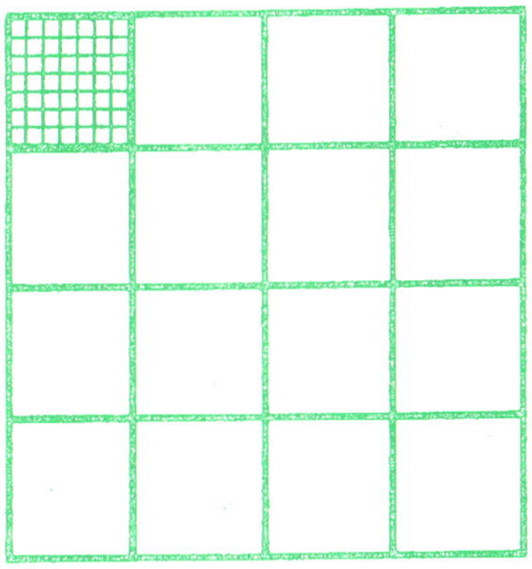

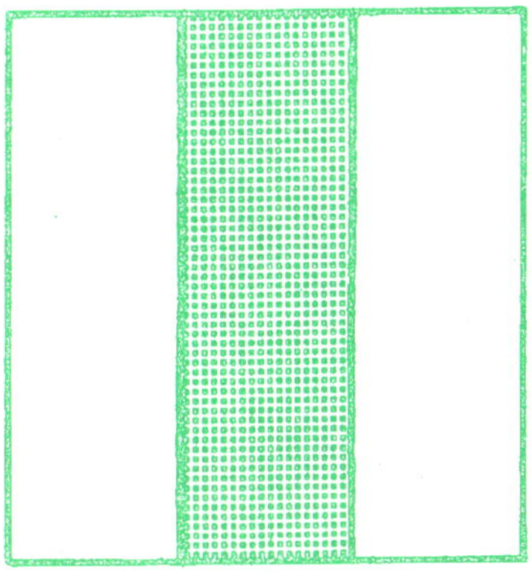

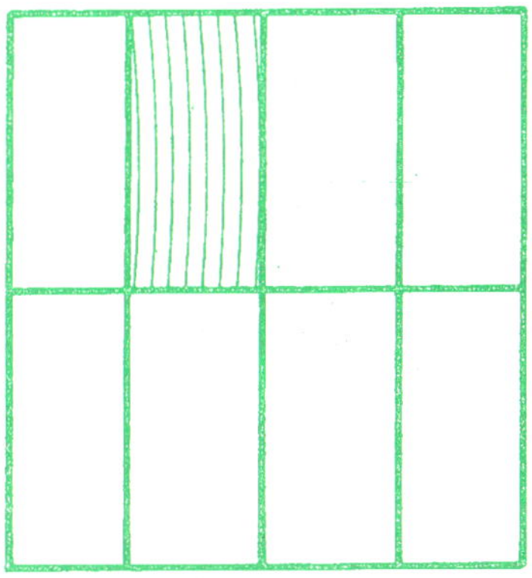

Ref: *Lab Sheet Annotations*, pages 142 and 144.

Name ______________________ Date ______________

Divide this box into <u>two</u> equal parts.

halves

Divide this box into <u>four</u> equal parts.

fourths

Divide this box into <u>eight</u> equal parts.

eighths

Ref: *Lab Sheet Annotations*, page 144.

Name ______________________ Date ______________

Use your rods for this:

$\frac{1}{2}$ of 2 = ☐

$\frac{1}{2}$ of 4 = ☐

$\frac{1}{2}$ of 6 = ☐

$\frac{1}{2}$ of 8 = ☐

$\frac{1}{2}$ of ◯ = ☐

$\frac{1}{2}$ of ◯ = ☐

$\frac{1}{2}$ of 20 = ☐

Ref: *Lab Sheet Annotations*, page 145.

Name ______________________ Date ______________

$\frac{1}{2} \times 4 = \square$

$\frac{1}{2} \times 6 = \square$

$\frac{1}{2} \times 10 = \square$

$\frac{1}{2} \times 8 = \square$

$\frac{1}{2} \times 2 = \square$

$\frac{1}{2} \times \bigcirc = \square$

$\frac{1}{2} \times \bigcirc = \square$

$\frac{1}{2} \times \bigcirc = \square$

$\frac{1}{2} \times \bigcirc = \square$

$\frac{1}{2} \times \bigcirc = \square$

Ref: *Lab Sheet Annotations*, page 145.

Which side has more wood?

Use rods.

Name ______________________

Date ____________________

Ref: *Lab Sheet Annotations*, page 200.

Name ______________________ Date ______________

< or > ?

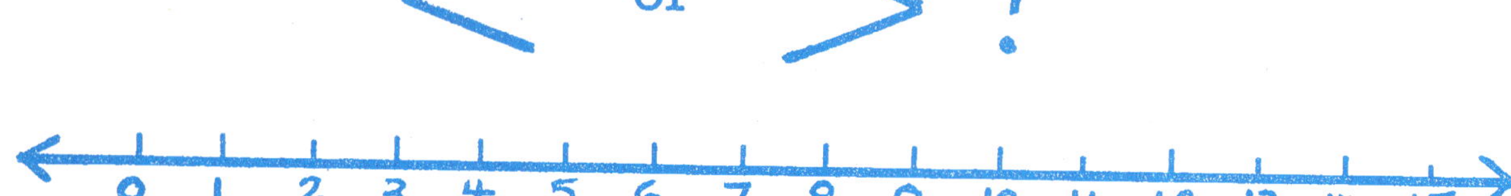

4 > 2 Four is greater than two.

4 < 5 Four is less than five.

7 < 8	5 4	4 7
7 > 3	5 6	5 7
7 12	18 5	7 7
7 6	0 5	9 7

7 < □	7 > □	□ < 10
8 < □	5 > □	□ < 2
10 < □	3 > □	2 < □
12 < □	3 < □	□ > 2

Ref: *Lab Sheet Annotations*, page 200.

Name ______________________ Date ______________

$5 > \square$

$1 > \square$

$\square > 3$

$\square > 11$

$9 = \square$

$\square = \square$

$\square = \square$

$\square > \bigcirc$

$3 + 5 > \square$

$3 + 5 = \square$

$6 - 2 > \square$

Ref: *Lab Sheet Annotations*, page 200.

Name ______________________ Date ______________

$25 > \square$

$25 = \square$

$\square > \bigcirc$

$15 = \square$

$\square = 3 \times 5$

$7 - 2 = \square$

$\square > 6 + 4$

$\square > 13$

$1 > \square$

$\square = \square$

Ref: *Lab Sheet Annotations*, page 200.

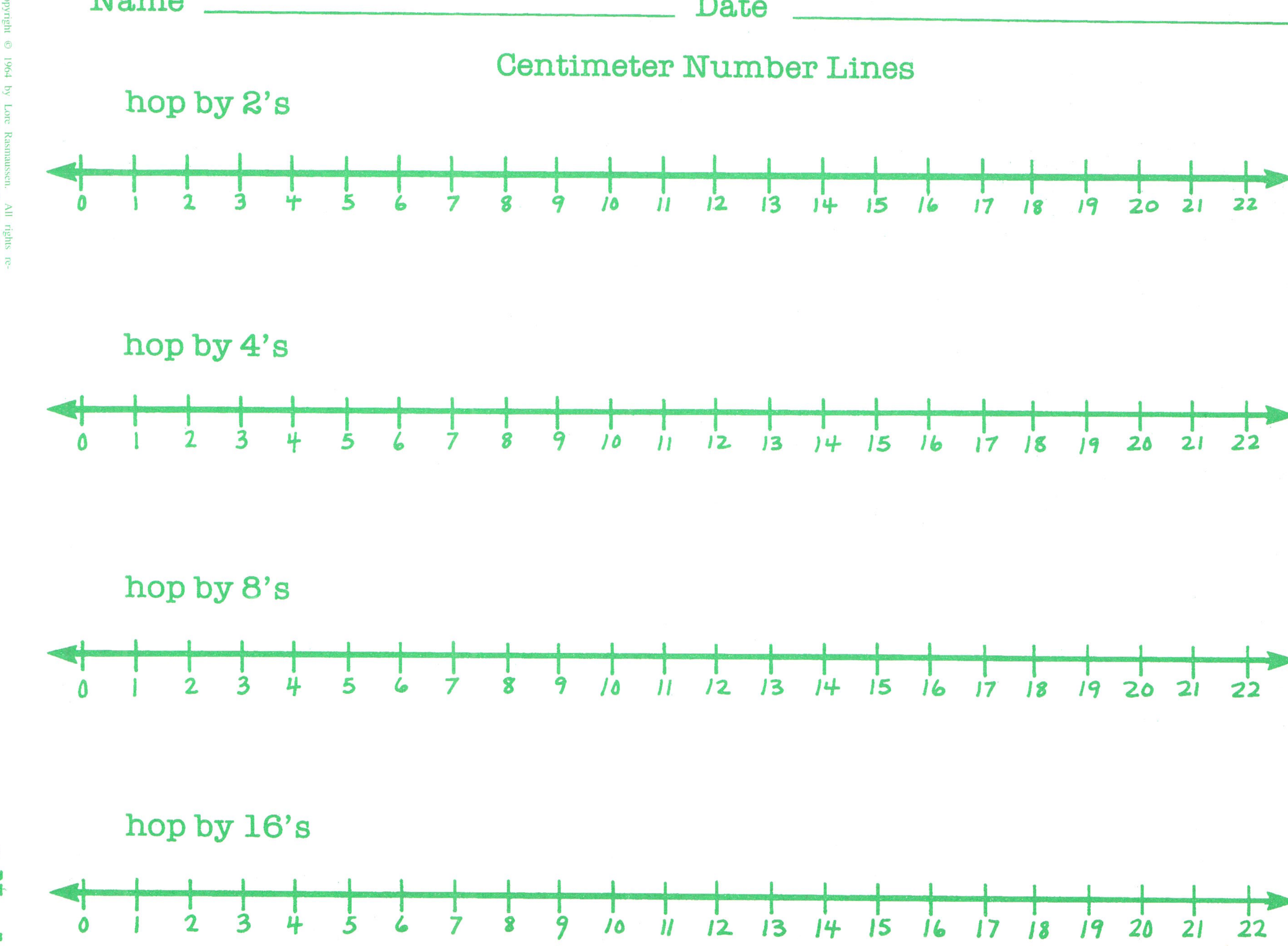

Ref: *Lab Sheet Annotations*, page 231.

Name ______________________ Date ______________

Ref: *Lab Sheet Annotations*, page 231.

Name ______________________ Date ______________

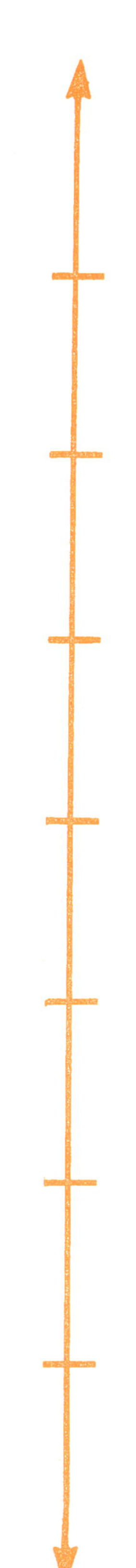

Ref: *Lab Sheet Annotations,* page 231.

Name ______________________ Date ______________

Ref: *Lab Sheet Annotations*, page 231.

Name ______________________ Date ______________

These are squares.

These are not squares.

Color all the squares.

Make some squares.

Ref: *Lab Sheet Annotations*, pages 283 and 284.

Name ______________________ Date ______________

These are triangles.

These are not triangles.

Color all triangles.

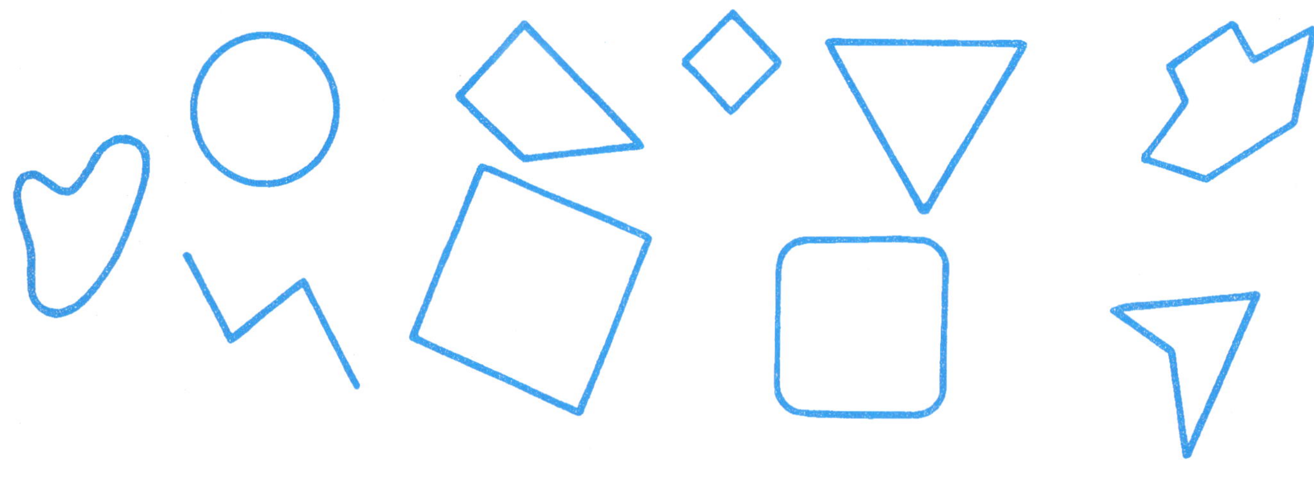

Make some triangles.

Ref: *Lab Sheet Annotations*, pages 283 and 284.

Name ______________________ Date ______________

These are polygons.

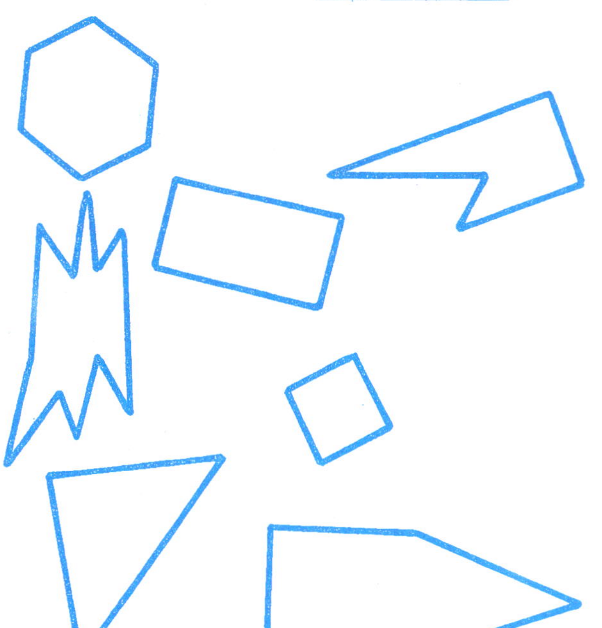

These are not polygons.

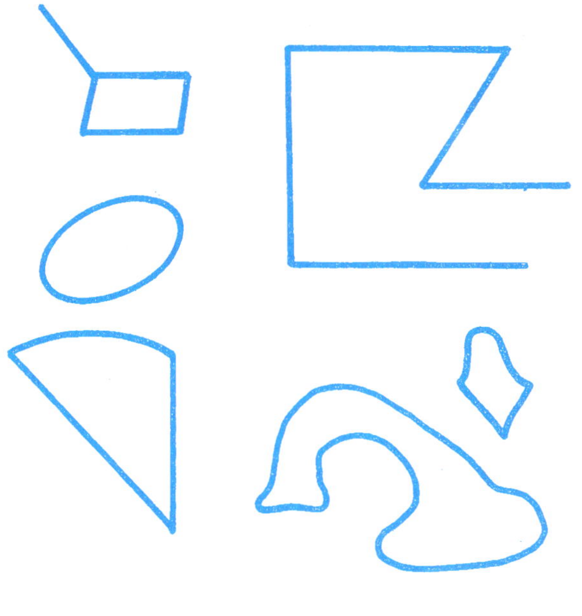

Color all polygons.

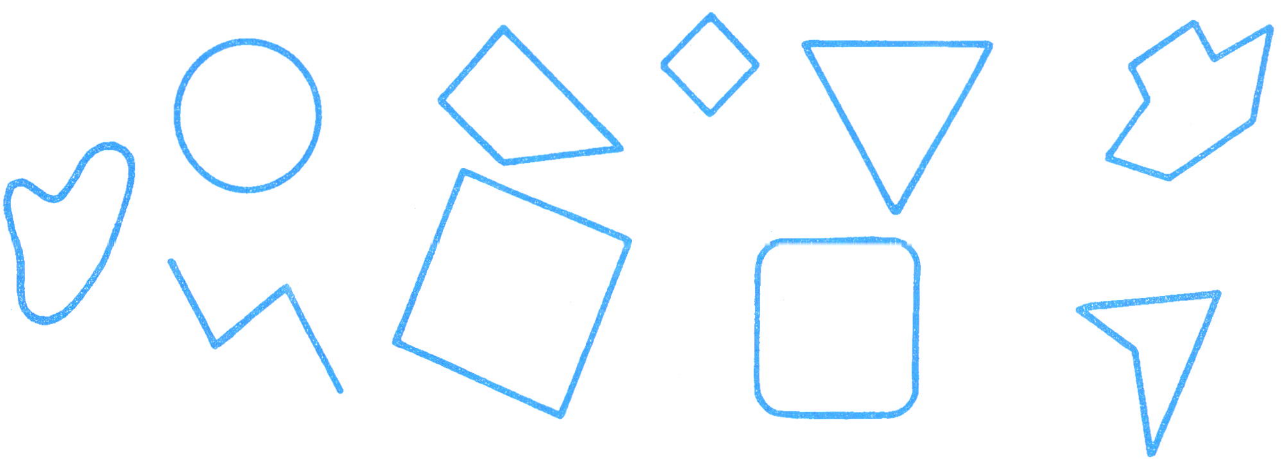

Make some polygons.

Ref: *Lab Sheet Annotations*, pages 283 and 285.

Name ______________________ Date ______________

Color red all four-sided polygons.
Color blue all six-sided polygons.
Color green all five-sided polygons.
Color black all three-sided polygons.

Ref: *Lab Sheet Annotations*, pages 283 and 285.

Name ______________________ Date ______________

Use a ruler and measure in centimeters.

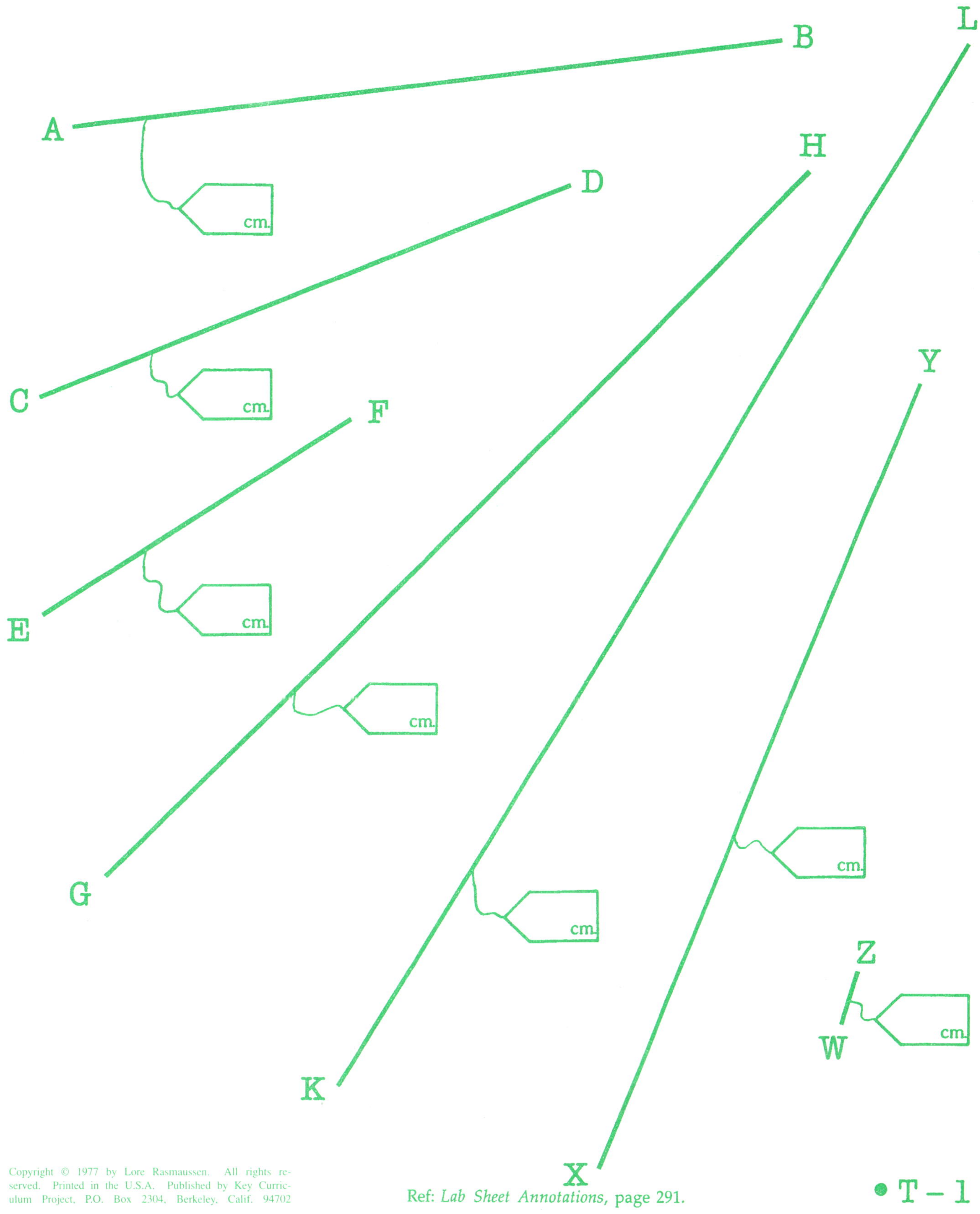

Ref: *Lab Sheet Annotations*, page 291.

Name ______________________ Date ______________

Use a ruler and measure in centimeters.

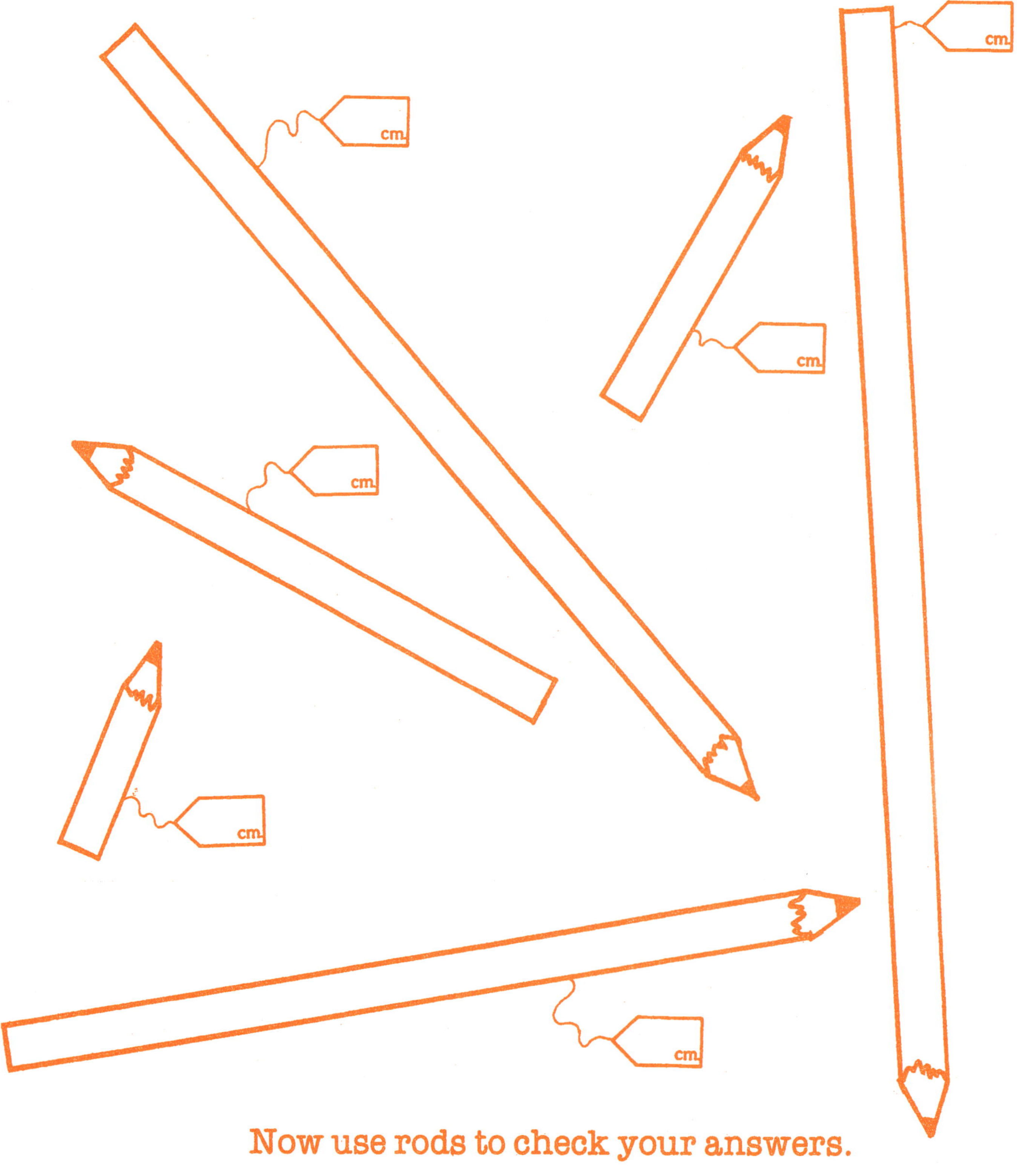

Now use rods to check your answers.

Ref: *Lab Sheet Annotations*, page 291.

Name ______________________ Date ______________

Use a ruler and measure in centimeters.

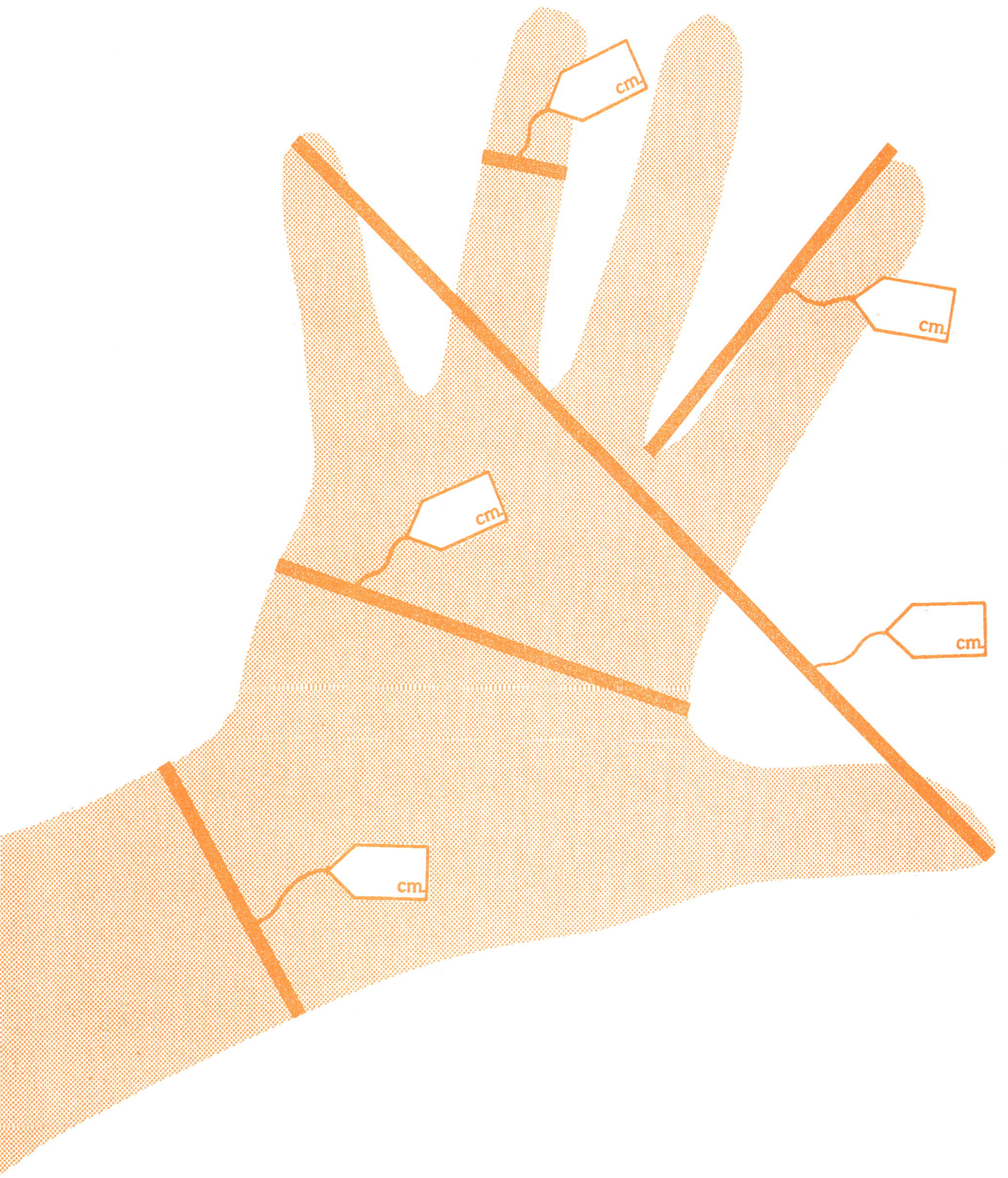

Ref: *Lab Sheet Annotations,* pages 291 and 292.

Name ______________________________ Date ____________________

My Hand

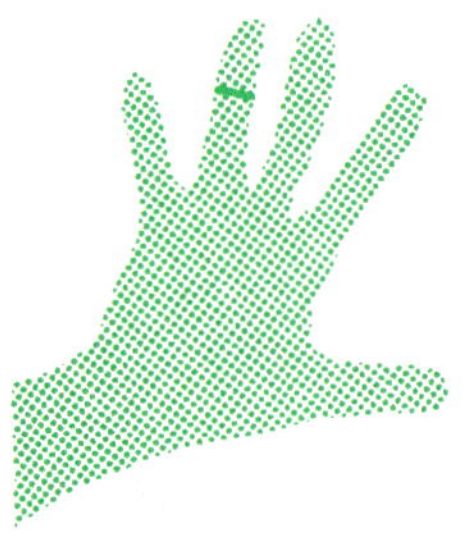

My finger is about ________ cm. wide.

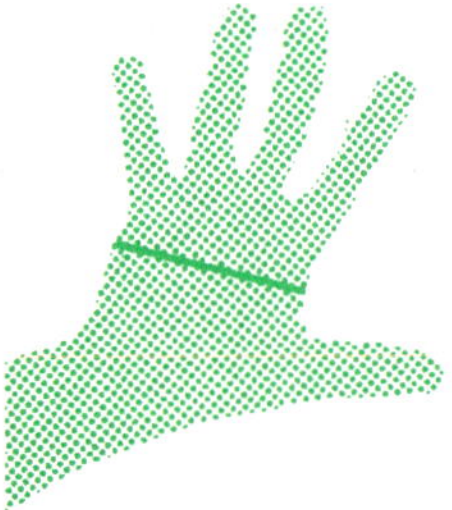

My palm is about ________ cm. wide.

My finger is about ________ cm. long.

My wrist is about ________ cm. wide.

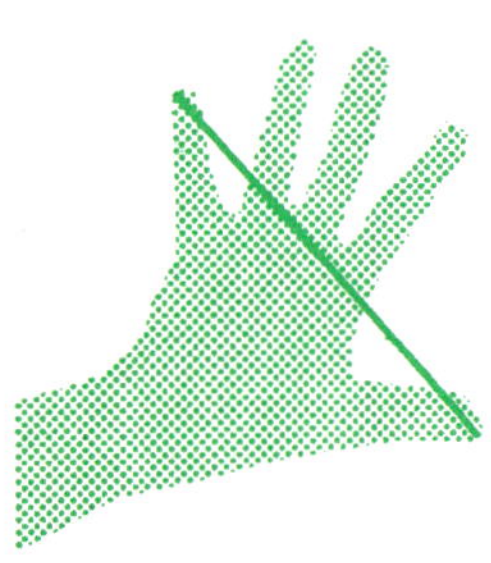

My hand span is about ________ cm.

Ref: *Lab Sheet Annotations*, pages 291 and 292.

Name ______________________ Date ______________________

Match.

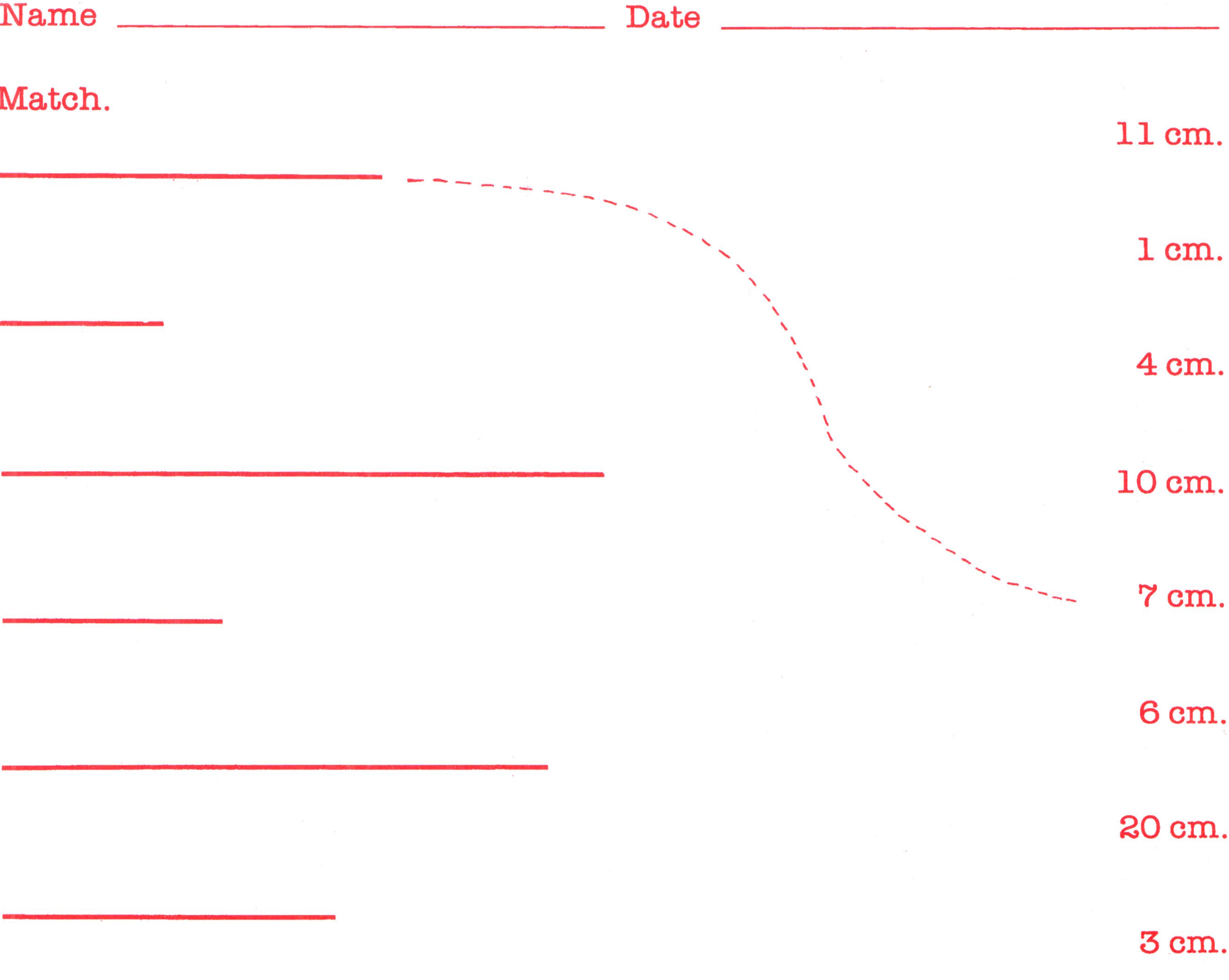

Ref: *Lab Sheet Annotations*, pages 291 and 293.

Name ____________________ Date ____________________

Use a centimeter ruler and draw these lines.

9 cm.

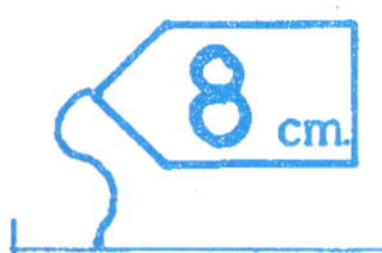

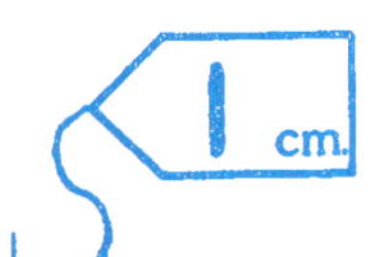

Ref: *Lab Sheet Annotations*, page 291.

Name ______________________ Date ______________

Use ruler. Measure in inches.

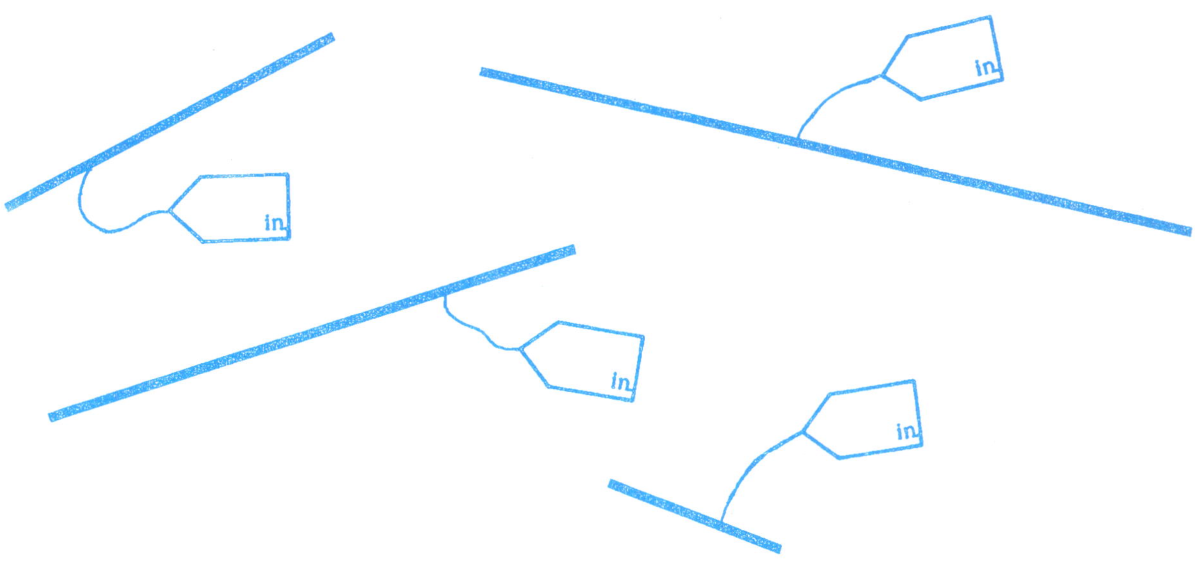

Make some more lines and measure them.

Ref: *Lab Sheet Annotations*, pages 291 and 295.

Name ______________________ Date ______________

Use an inch ruler and draw these lines.

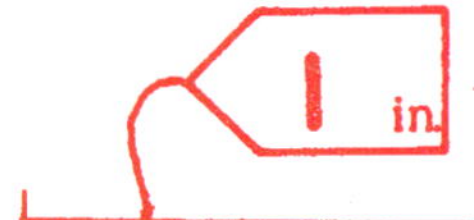

 Published by Key Curriculum Project, P.O. Box 2304, Berkeley, Calif. 94702

Ref: *Lab Sheet Annotations*, pages 291 and 295.

Name ______________________ Date ______________

Find the length and width.

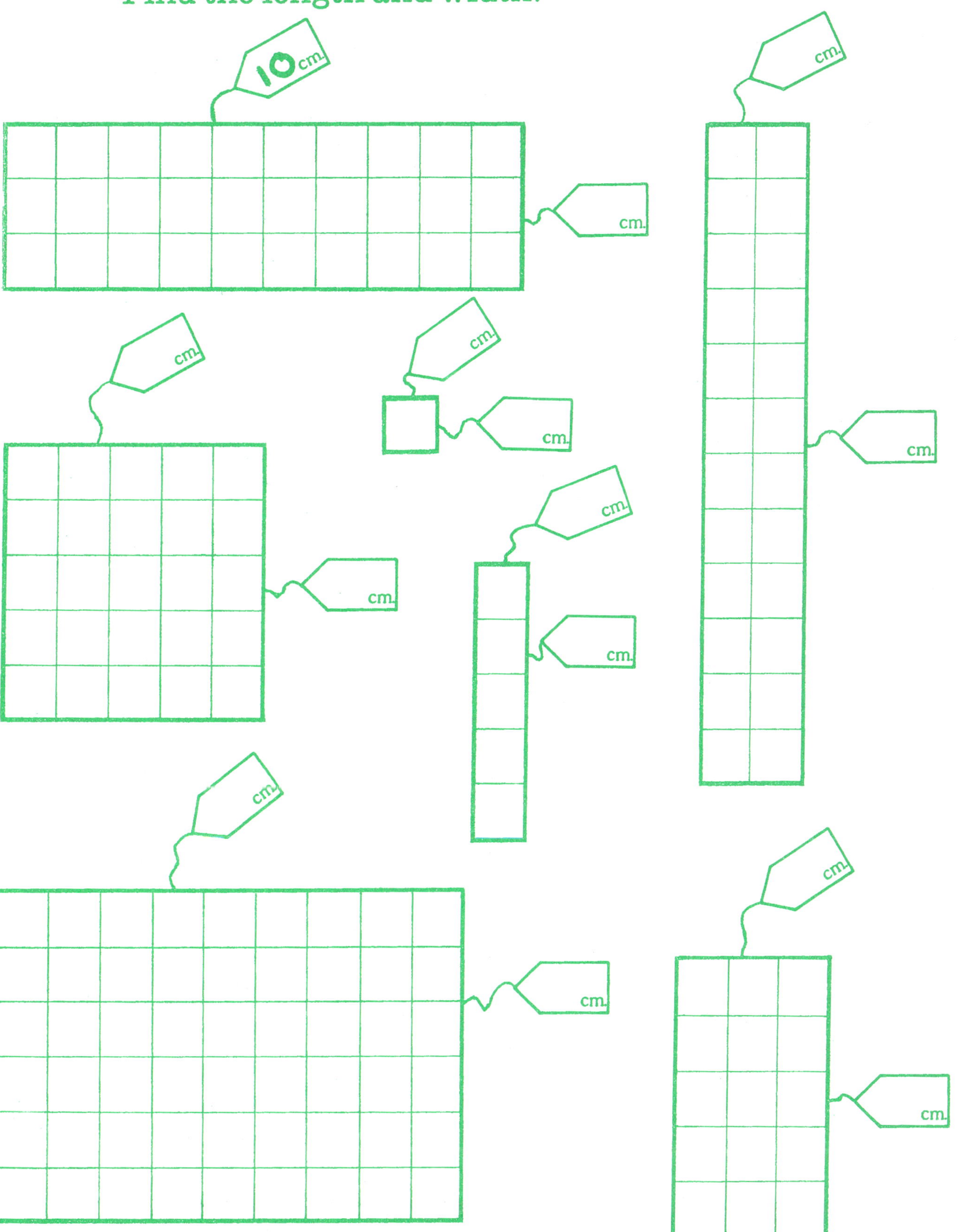

Ref: *Lab Sheet Annotations*, page 295.

Name ______________________ Date ______________

Use the rods to find the length and width.

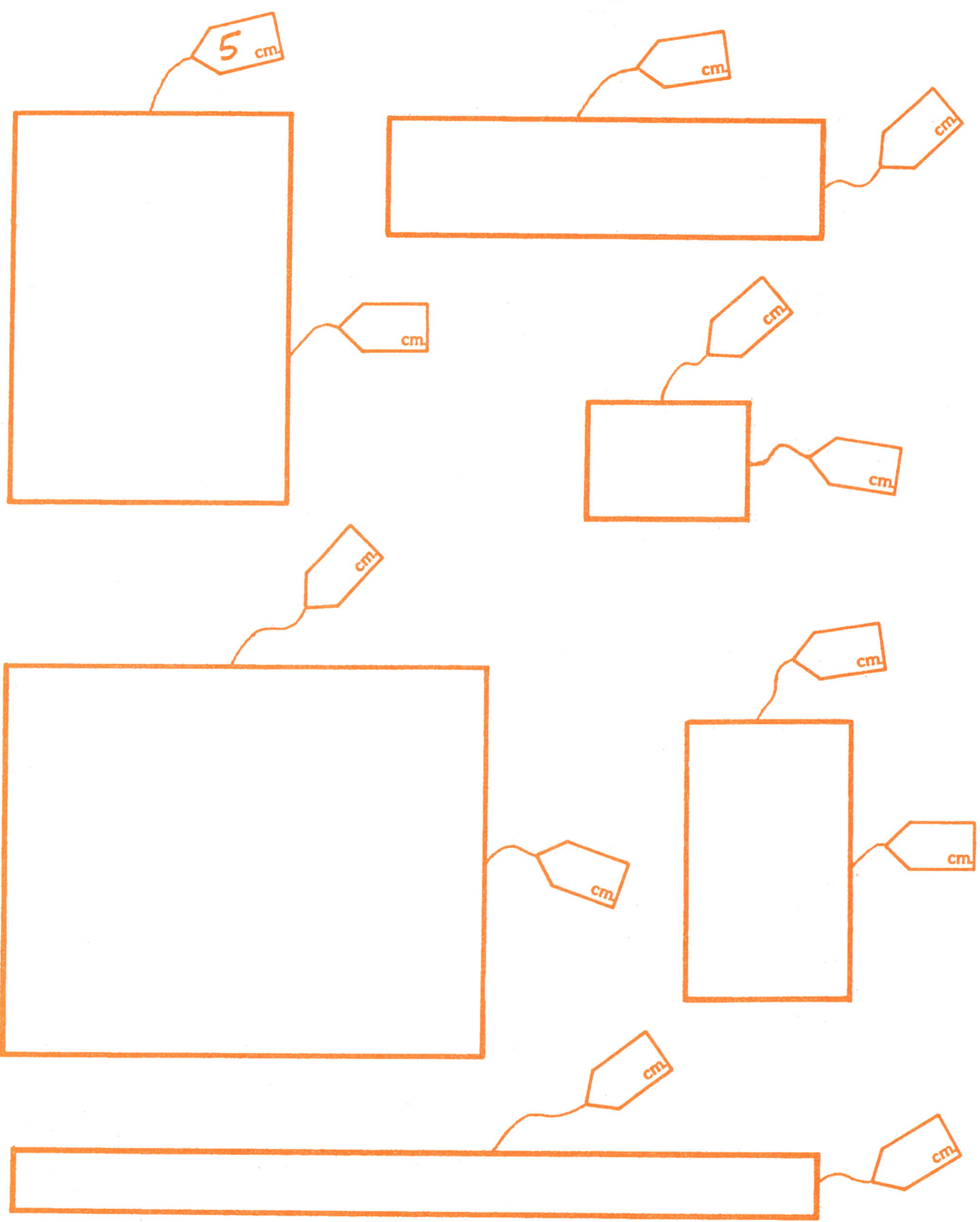

Ref: *Lab Sheet Annotations*, page 295.

Name ______________________ Date ______________

How many square centimeters?

1 sq.cm

30 sq.cm

sq.cm

sq.cm

sq.cm

sq.cm

sq.cm

Ref: *Lab Sheet Annotations*, page 295.

Name ______________________ Date ______________

How many square centimeters?

Use your rods.

Ref: *Lab Sheet Annotations*, page 295.

Name ______________________ Date ______________

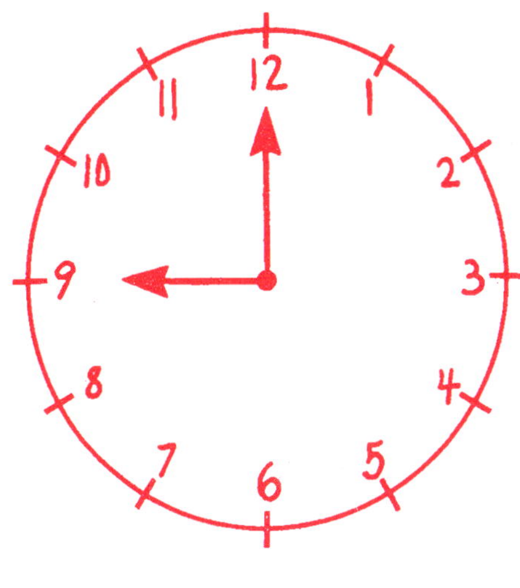

______

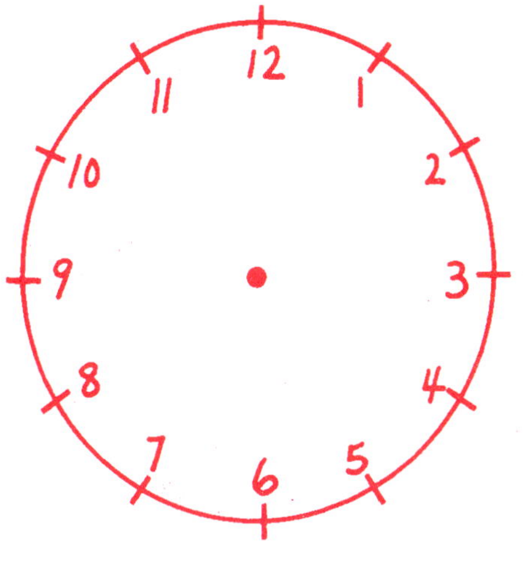

2:00

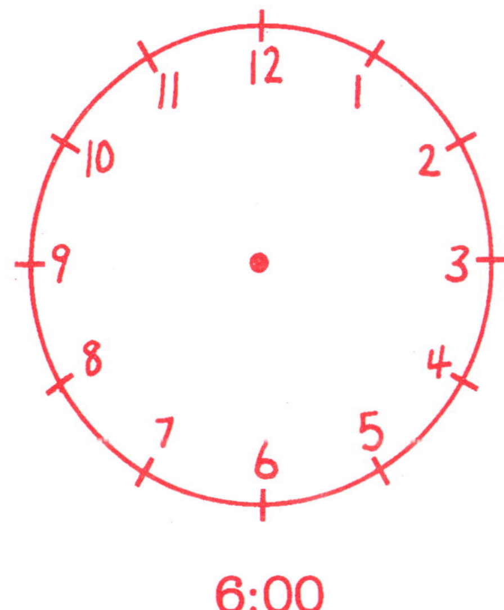

6:00

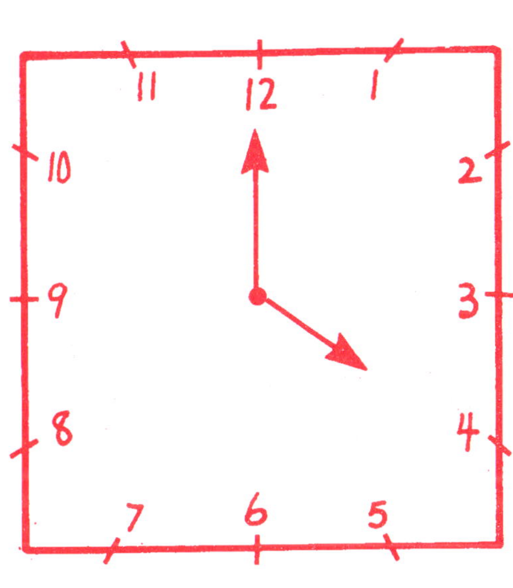

______

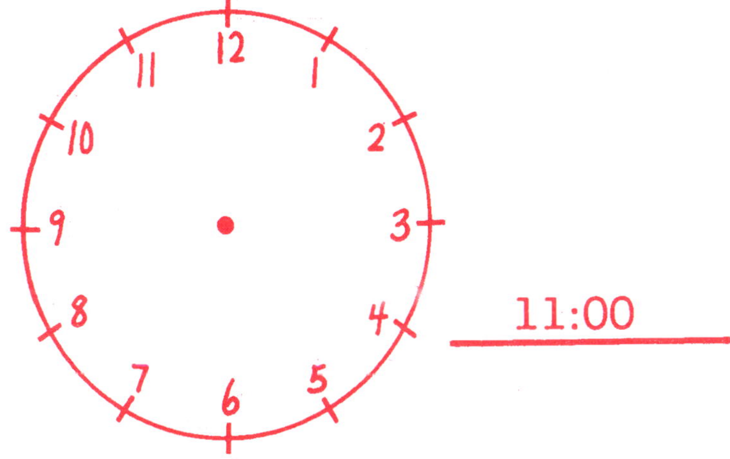

11:00

Ref: *Lab Sheet Annotations*, page 333.

Name ______________________ Date ______________

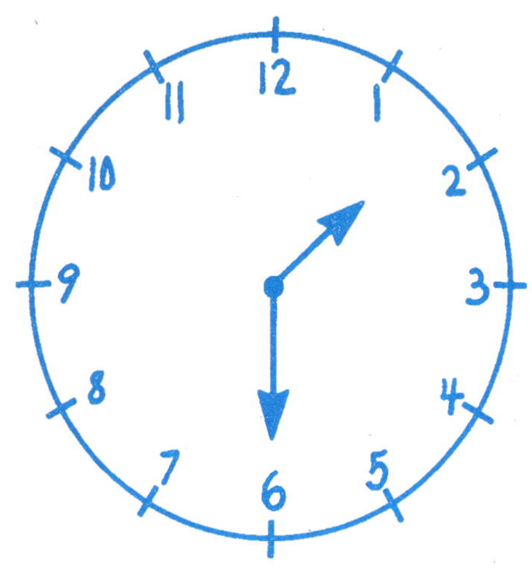

This is 1:30

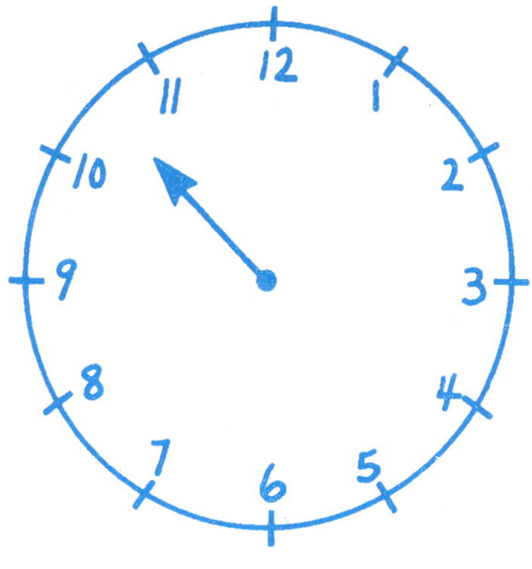

______ :30

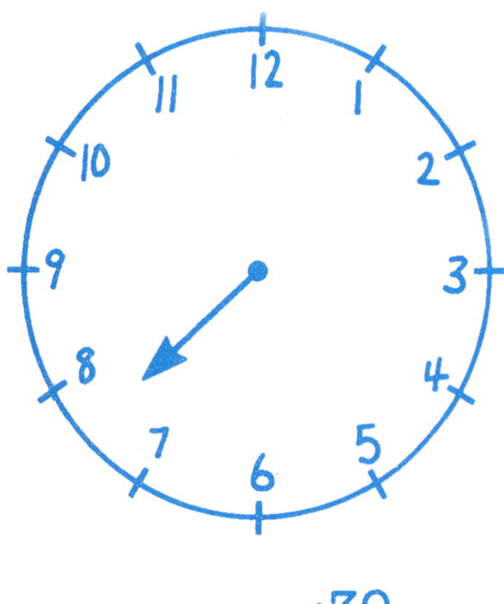

______ :30

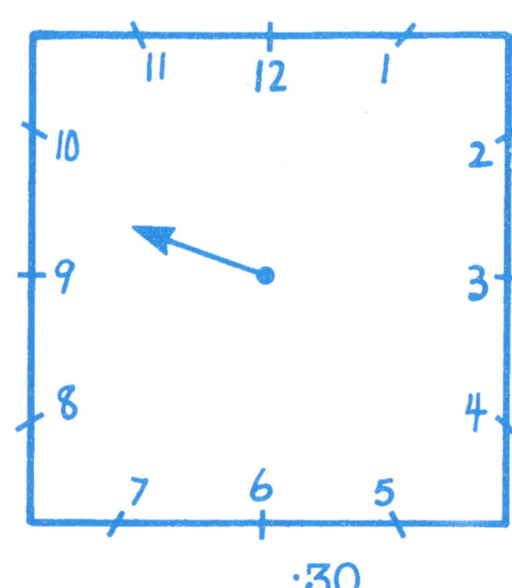

______ :30

4:30

Ref: *Lab Sheet Annotations*, page 333.

Name ____________________ Date ____________

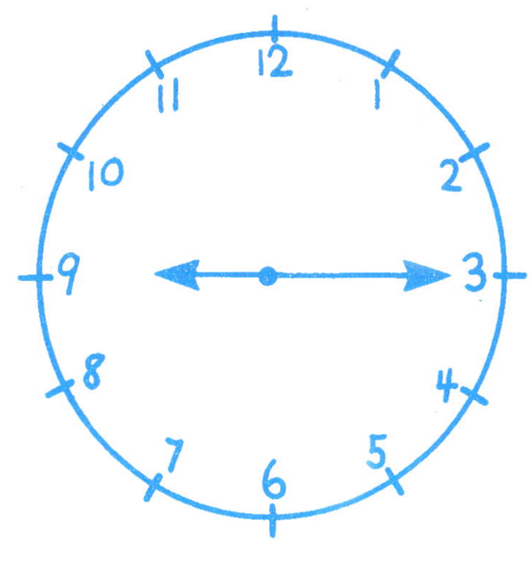

This is 9:15

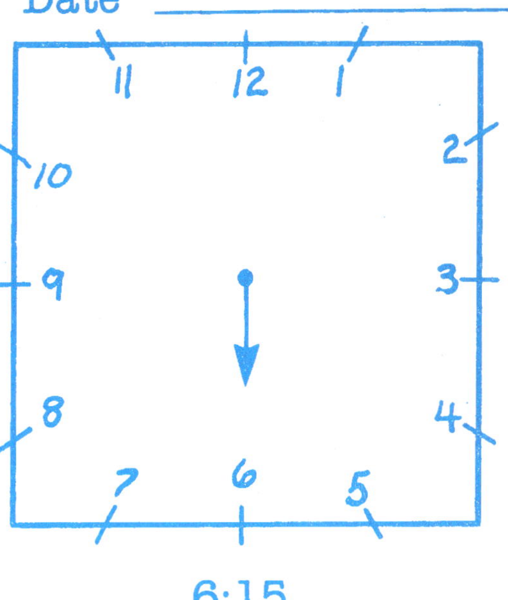

6:15

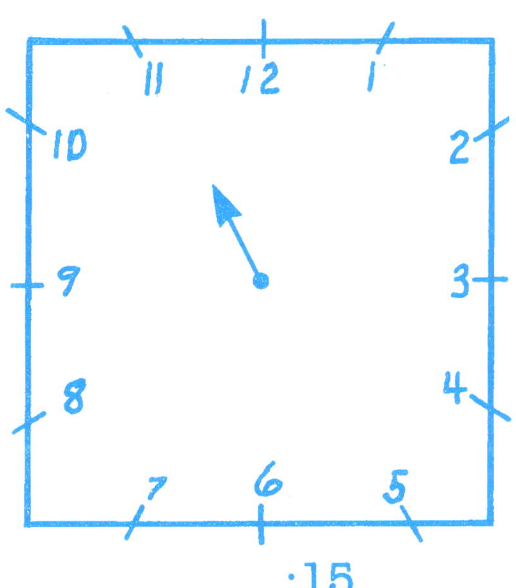

:15

____

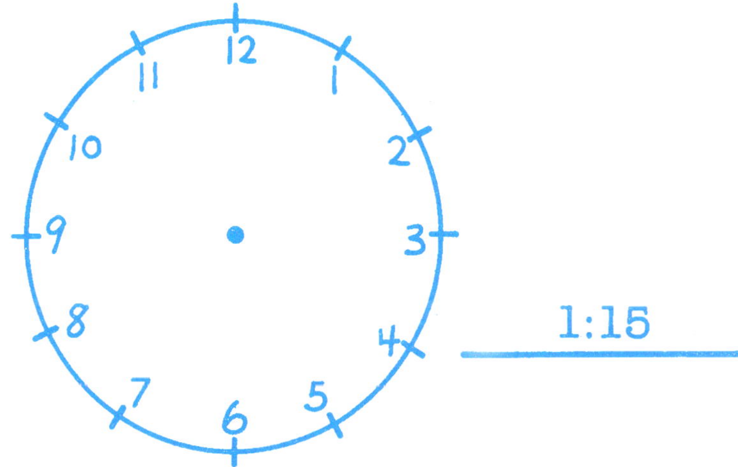

1:15

Ref: *Lab Sheet Annotations*, page 333.

Name ______________________ Date ______________

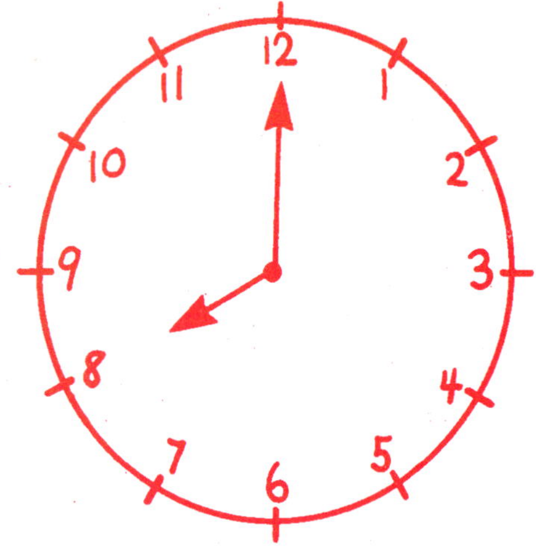

______

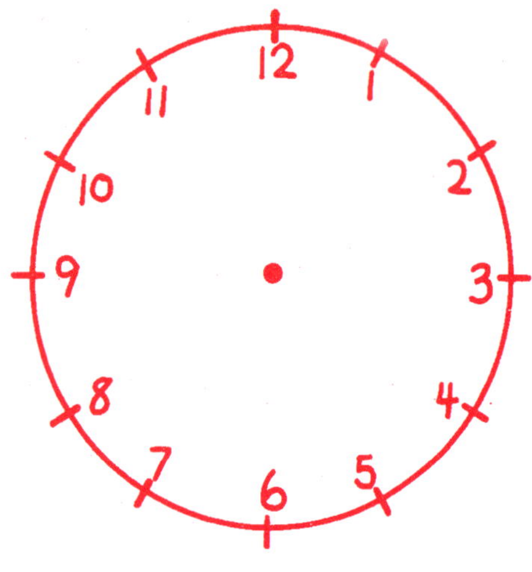

9:30

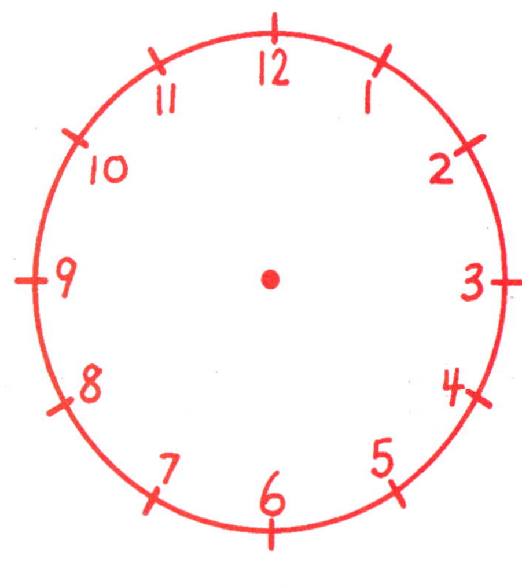

______

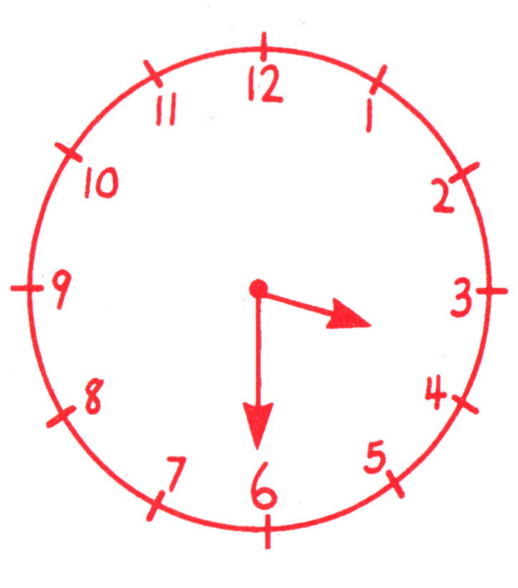

______

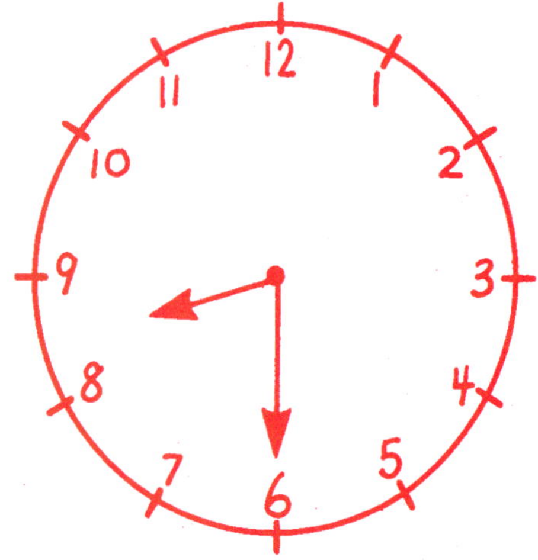

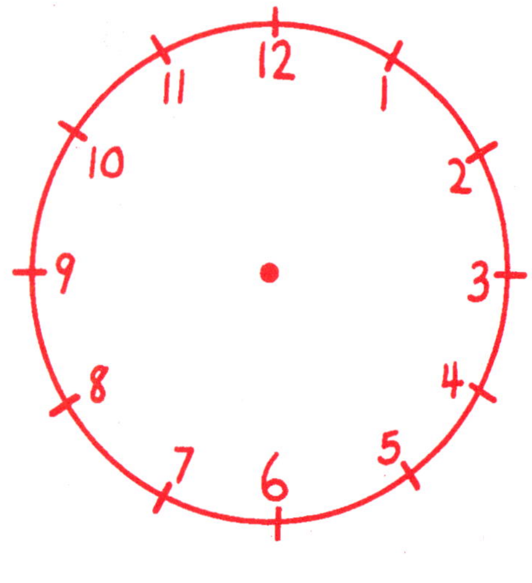

5:00

Ref: *Lab Sheet Annotations*, page 333.

Name ______________________ Date ______________________

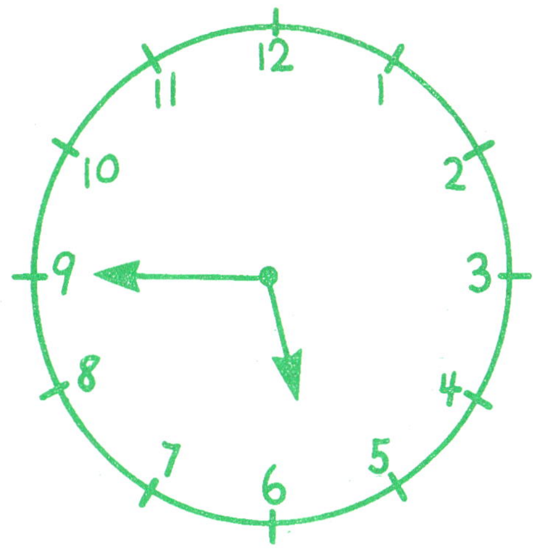

This is 5:45

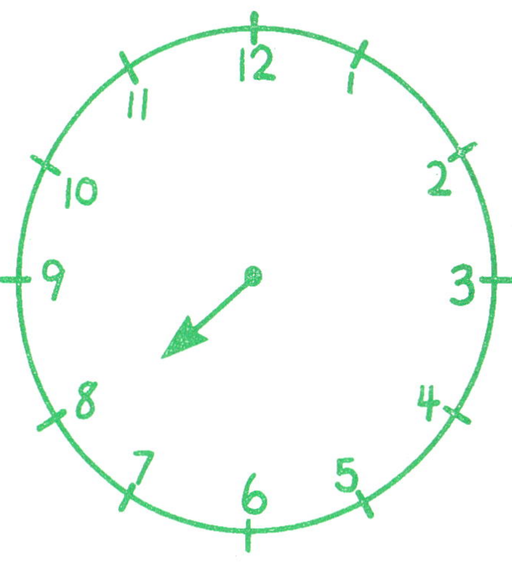

7:45

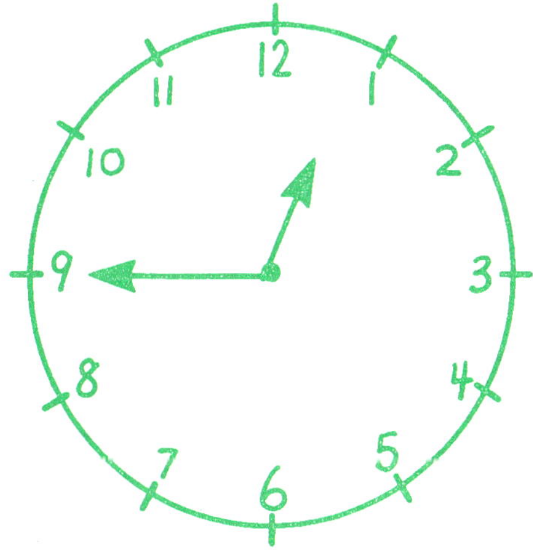

____

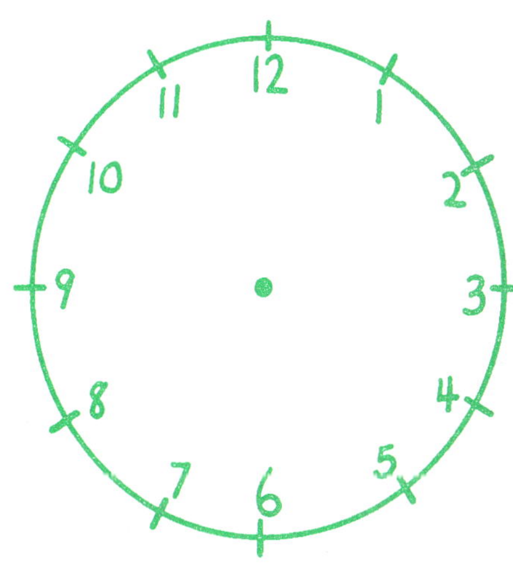

3:45

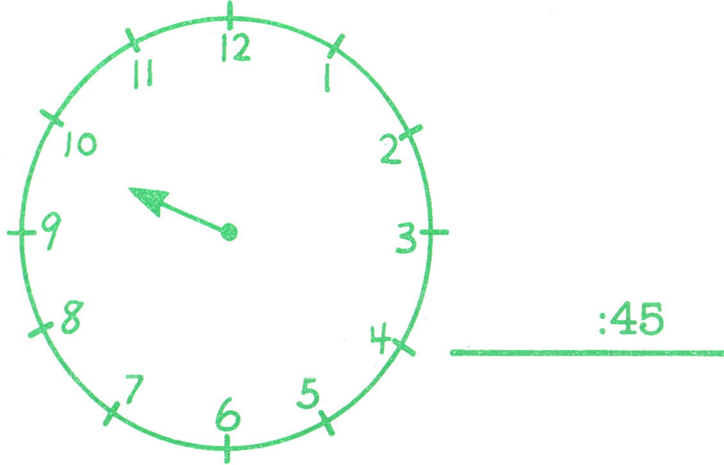

:45

Ref: *Lab Sheet Annotations*, page 333.

Name ____________________ Date ____________________

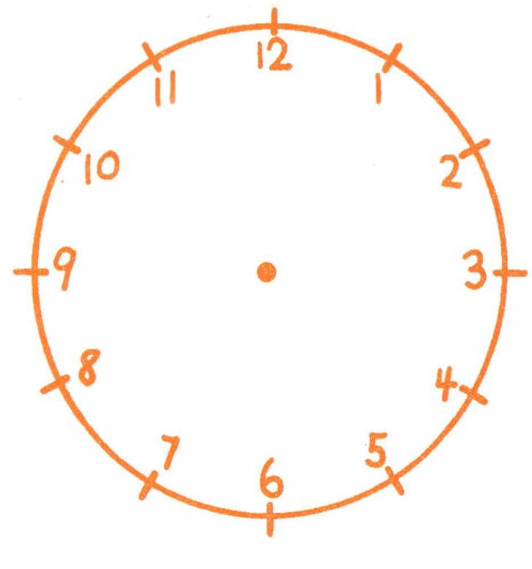

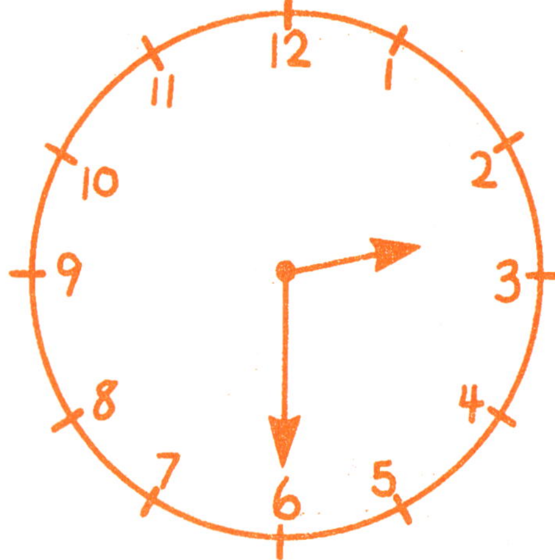

11:45

______

11 12 1 2 3 4 5 6 7 8 9 10

:15

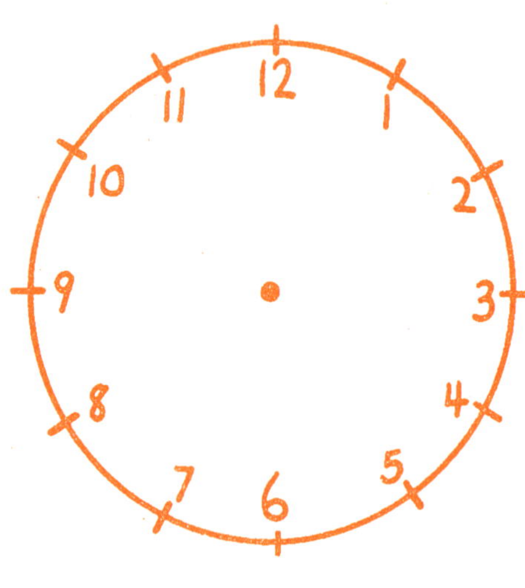

7:00

11 12 1 2 3 4 5 6 7 8 9 10

4: ______

Ref: *Lab Sheet Annotations*, page 333.

Name ____________________ Date ____________

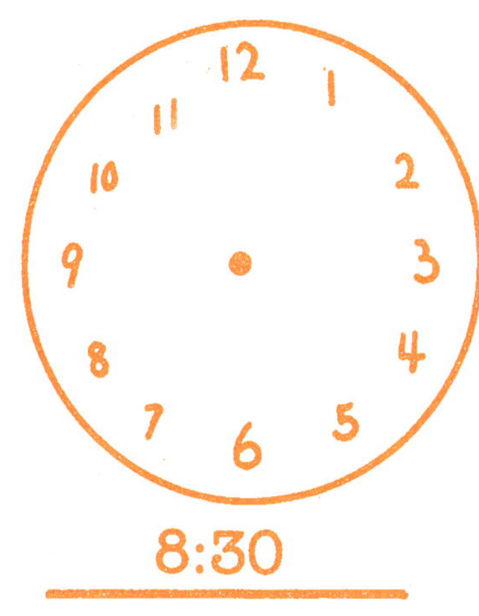

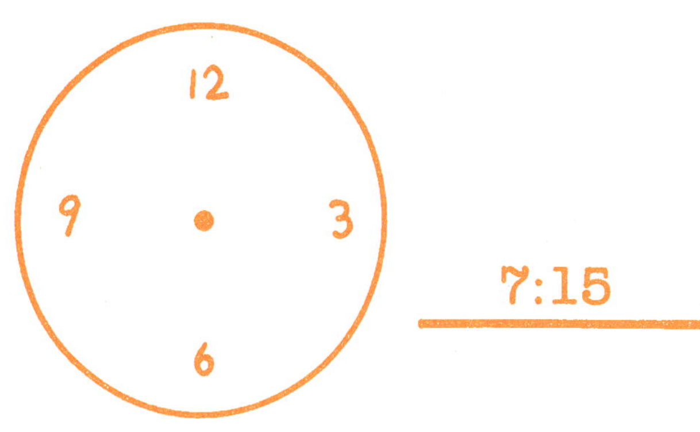

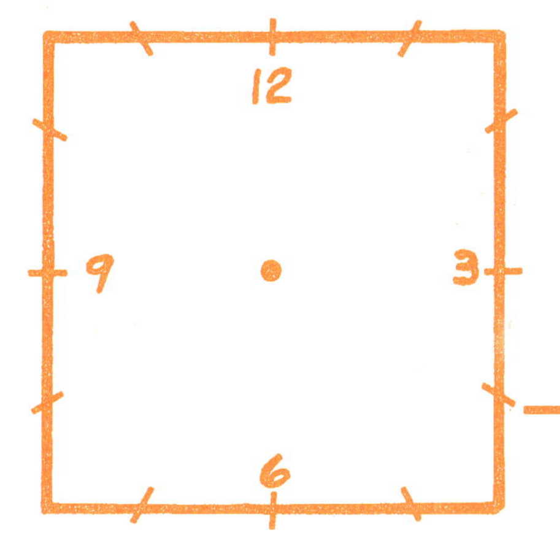

2:15

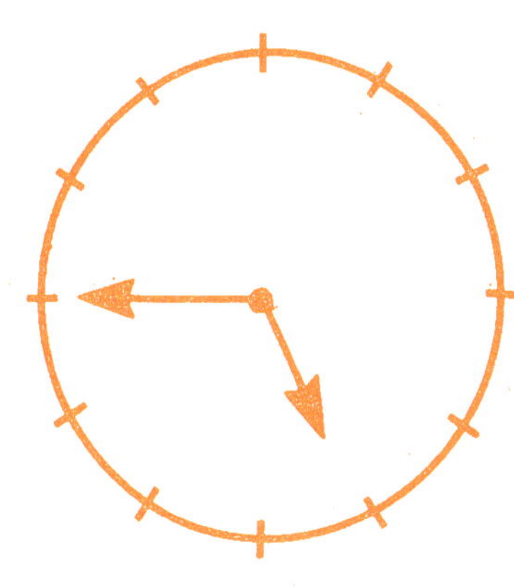

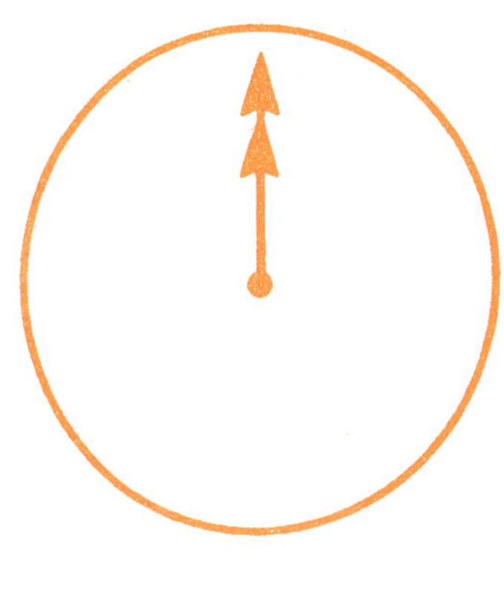

Ref: *Lab Sheet Annotations*, page 333.

Name ____________________ Date ____________________

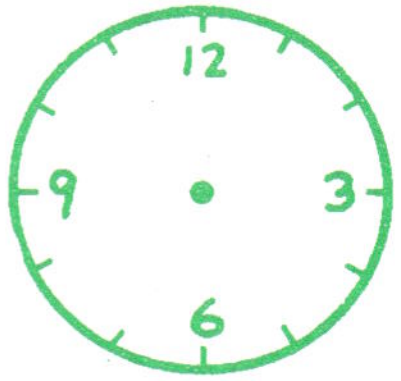

Pat gets up at 7:30.	Pat eats at 8:00.
Pat goes to school at 8:15.	School starts at 8:30.
Pat goes out to play at 10:45.	Pat has arithmetic at ________ .

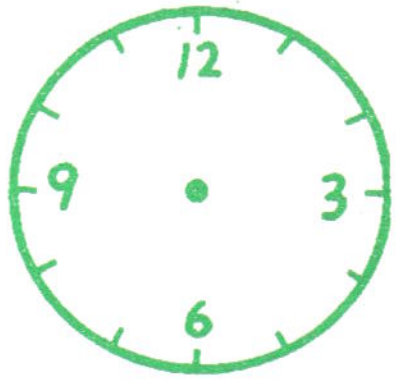

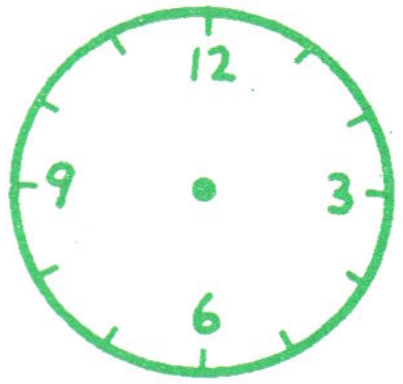

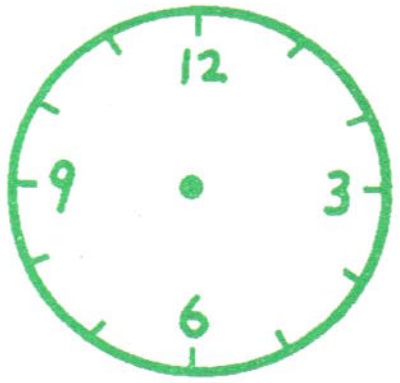

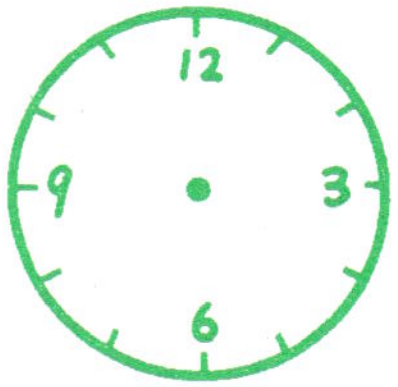

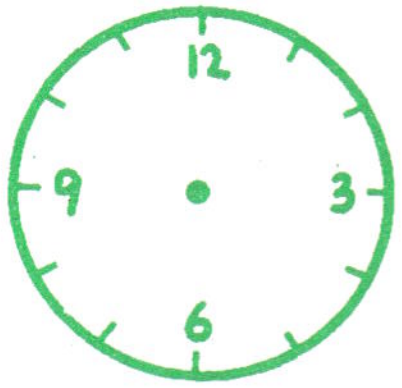

 Published by Key Curriculum Project, P.O. Box 2304, Berkeley, Calif. 94702

Ref: *Lab Sheet Annotations*, page 335.

Name ______________________ Date ______________________

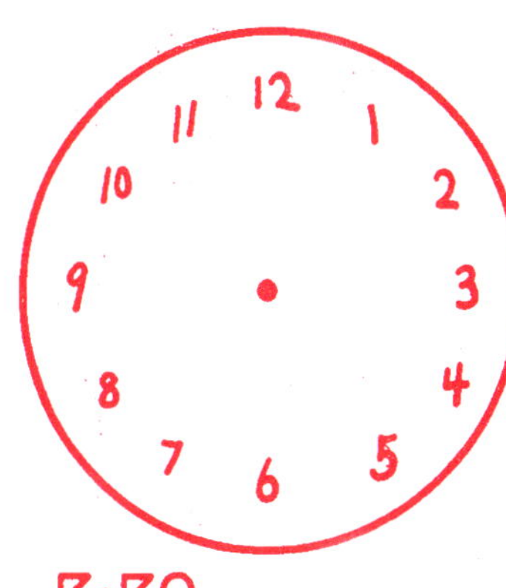

3:30

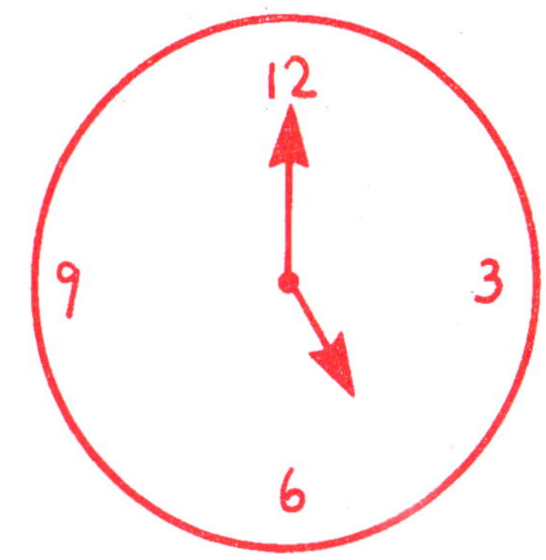

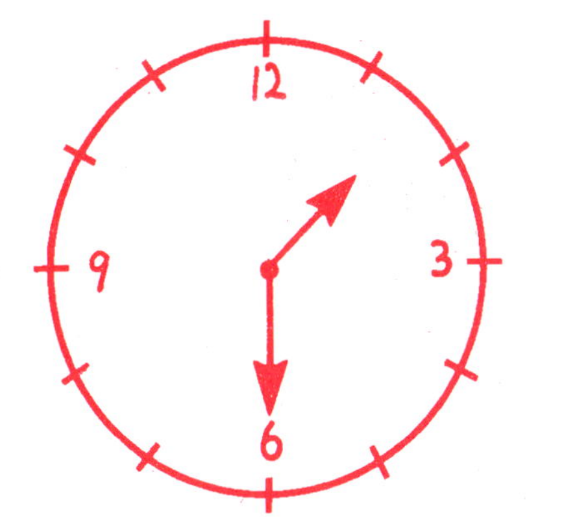

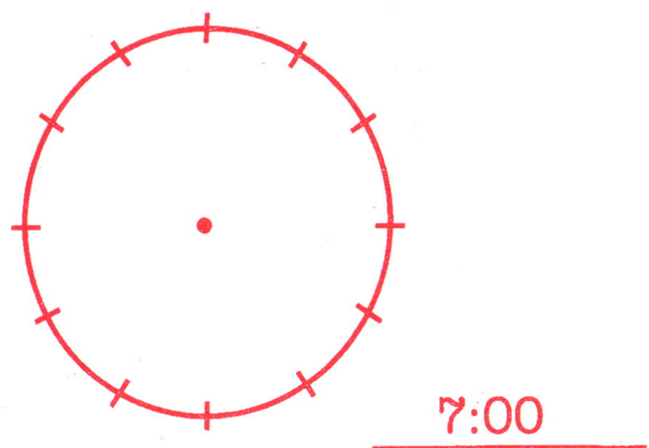

7:00

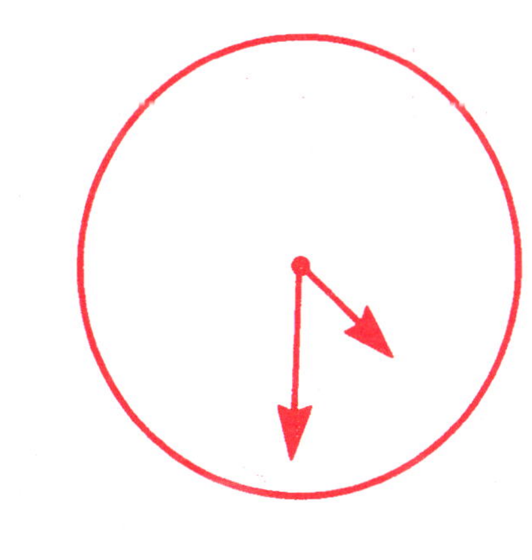

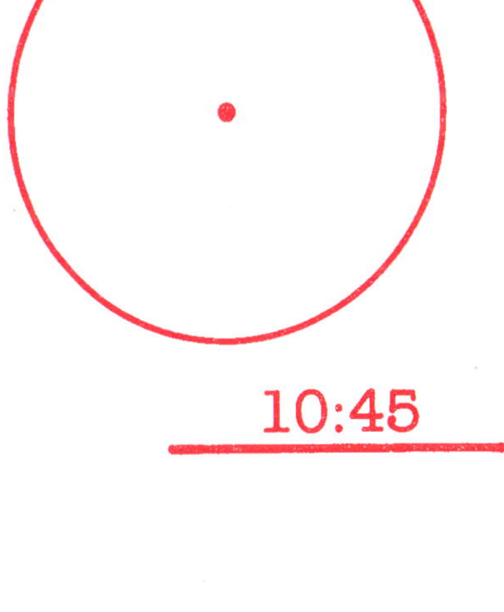

10:45

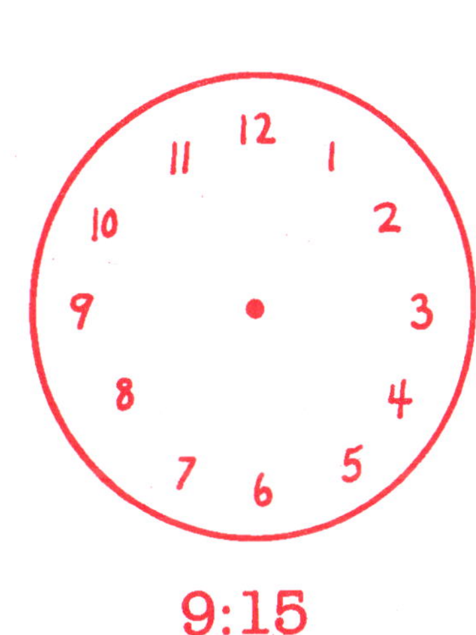

9:15

Ref: *Lab Sheet Annotations*, page 333.

Name ______________________ Date ______________

The fork is at ____ o'clock.

The glass is at ____ o'clock.

The spoon is at ____ o'clock.

The peas on the plate are at ____ o'clock.

Put some mashed potatoes on the plate at 12 o'clock.

Ref: *Lab Sheet Annotations*, page 336.